THE MANAGEM
CHILDREN V
EMOTIONAL ᵃₙᵤ
BEHAVIOURAL
DIFFICULTIES

THE MANAGEMENT OF CHILDREN WITH EMOTIONAL AND BEHAVIOURAL DIFFICULTIES

EDITED BY VED P. VARMA

ROUTLEDGE
London and New York

This book is dedicated, by the
editor, with affection and
esteem, to Dr. S. K. and
Mary Roy

First published 1990 by Routledge
11 New Fetter Lane, London EC4P 4EE

Simultaneously published in the USA and Canada
by Routledge
a division of Routledge, Chapman and Hall, Inc.
29 West 35th Street, New York, NY 10001

©1990 Ved P. Varma for the whole collection; the copyright for each
chapter shall remain with the contributors.

Phototypeset by Input Typesetting Ltd, London

Printed and bound in Great Britain by
Billings & Sons Limited, Worcester

British Library Cataloguing in Publication Data

The management of children with emotional and
behavioural difficulties.
1. Maladjusted children
I. Varma, Ved P. (Ved prakash)
362.7'4

ISBN 0-415-02245-2
0-415-02246-0 (Pbk)

CONTENTS

List of Contributors   vii

Introduction   ix
Ved P. Varma

1 EMOTIONAL AND BEHAVIOURAL DIFFICULTIES
(EBD): SOME GENERAL POINTS   1
Robin Higgins

2 THE PSYCHODYNAMIC THEORY OF CHILDREN
WITH EMOTIONAL AND BEHAVIOURAL
DIFFICULTIES   18
Christopher Dare

3 BEHAVIOURAL APPROACHES TO THE
MANAGEMENT OF CHILDREN WITH EMOTIONAL
AND BEHAVIOURAL DIFFICULTIES   41
Jean E. Sambrooks

4 THE PSYCHIATRIC EXAMINATION OF CHILDREN
WITH EMOTIONAL AND BEHAVIOURAL
DIFFICULTIES   58
Philip Barker

5 PSYCHOLOGICAL ASSESSMENT AND THE
MANAGEMENT OF CHILDREN WITH EMOTIONAL
AND BEHAVIOURAL DIFFICULTIES   79
David Jones

6 THE PSYCHOANALYTIC PSYCHOTHERAPY OF
  CHILDREN WITH EMOTIONAL AND BEHAVIOURAL
  DIFFICULTIES   96
  Francis M. J. Dale

7 RESISTANCE AND CO-OPERATION: THE NEED FOR
  BOTH   115
  A Further Study of Psychotherapy in a Day Unit
  Dilys Daws

8 WORKING WITH THE FAMILIES OF CHILDREN
  WITH EMOTIONAL AND BEHAVIOURAL
  DIFFICULTIES   137
  Gillian Miles

9 THE MANAGEMENT OF CHILDREN WITH
  EMOTIONAL AND BEHAVIOURAL DIFFICULTIES
  IN ORDINARY AND SPECIAL SCHOOLS   154
  Colin J. Smith

Contributors' Addresses   170

Name Index   172

Subject Index   174

CONTRIBUTORS

Dr Philip Barker
MB BS FRCP (Ed) FRC Psych FRCP (C)
Professor of Psychiatry and Paediatrics, University of Calgary
Psychiatrist, Alberta Children's Hospital

Francis M. J. Dale
Principal Child Psychotherapist
Child Guidance Clinic, Torquay

Dr Christopher Dare
MB FRCPsych MRCP DPM
Consultant Psychiatrist
Bethlem Royal and Maudsley Hospital, London,
Senior Lecturer, Department of Psychiatry, Institute of Psychiatry,
University of London

Dilys Daws
Principal Child Psychotherapist
The Tavistock Clinic, London

Dr Robin Higgins
Former Consultant Child and Family Psychiatrist,
Richmond-upon-Thames

Dr David Jones
PhD
Lecturer, Department of Psychology
Birkbeck College, University of London

Gillian Miles
Social Worker
Child and Family Department
The Tavistock Clinic, London

Jean E. Sambrooks
BA MSc ABPsS
Top Grade Clinical Psychologist
Department of Clinical Psychology
Royal Liverpool Children's Hospital

Colin J. Smith
Lecturer in Special Education
The University of Birmingham

Dr Ved P. Varma
PhD (London)
Former Educational Psychologist
London Boroughs of Richmond-upon-Thames
and Brent

INTRODUCTION

As is well known, the management of children with emotional and behavioural difficulties has always been a source of worry and anguish to those who have to deal with them because many such children are unpredictable and sometimes embarrassing. Worst of all, some of them can make us feel helpless. This is why we need to know more about them – about how they think, feel, or behave.

This interesting symposium is an excellent account of the management of such children. The contributors include three psychiatrists, two psychologists, two psychotherapists, an educationist, and a social worker – all of whom are recognized authorities in their respective subjects. Accordingly their views command every respect.

I would, therefore, wholeheartedly recommend this inspired, jargon-free, and pleasant book to readers concerned with children in any way. In particular, students of psychiatry, psychology, psychotherapy, education, and social work will find within it much to help them in their first encounters with child patients. The caring professionals, too, might like to read this competent book, with a critical eye, relating it to the way in which the contributors present their cases.

I hope every reader will take the book for what it is worth and throughout compare it with the fruits of his or her own wisdom and experience. Finally, may those who read this book come to realize that the world belongs to those who work for the suffering. And that the suffering children teach us most about the human mind and mental health.

The Editor would like to thank the reader for taking the trouble to read this book. As regards my colleagues and contributors, it is impossible to express my deep gratitude in words – it is implied in working in partnership with them in this context.

Ved P. Varma
October 1988

Chapter One

EMOTIONAL AND BEHAVIOURAL DIFFICULTIES (EBD): SOME GENERAL POINTS

ROBIN HIGGINS

EBD AND MALADJUSTMENT

The descriptive group of Children with Emotional and Behavioural Disorders (*sic*) received formal recognition in the Report on Special Educational Needs published in 1978.[1] In the Report, the EBD group was laid alongside the following nine other groups: visual and hearing disabilities, physically handicapped, children with epilepsy, children with speech and language disorders, children with specific learning difficulties, and with mild, moderate, and severe learning difficulties (paras 11.21–11.64).

The first point to bear in mind about the Report and the group for which the document provides a context is that its primary purpose was to define and quantify special educational needs and to point up ways of meeting these needs. The language 'game', in Wittgenstein's sense,[2] being played in the Report has an organizational and administrative basis with a firm focus on education. The Report was associated with educational legislation. Indeed, Report and legislation represented a more extensive version of a similar exercise carried out some 30 years earlier around the time of and subsequent to the Education Act of 1944.[3] In those earlier days, the category equivalent to EBD was Maladjustment.

It is important to understand this background if EBD as a category is to make much sense; for taken at face value, the amalgamation of 'emotion' and 'behaviour' presents major problems of logical definition. In the first place the two terms have proved over the centuries notoriously hard to pin down.[4] Are emotions primarily instinctive libidinal drives (whatever we mean by that)? What is their relation to sensuality on one side and the higher sentiments on the other? Does behaviour include inner conscious states which

1

may not necessarily erupt in any clear physical manifestation but which may be a determining force in a human organism's subsequent response?

In the second place, however defined, there is such a degree of overlap in the two phenomena that psychologists and others have been persistently side-tracked into controversy as to whether emotions should be subsumed by or subsume behaviour.[5]

In the third place, again at face value, the setting of EBD on a par with learning difficulties, physical handicaps, and so on raises a long-recognized possibility of a category mistake (in the logical linguistic sense) similar to that of setting a more abstract general concept such as a university on a par with the more concrete instances such as colleges which go to make up the collective term. Children falling into the other nine categories are quite likely to include a degree of EBD in their needs. The converse is much less likely. There is not the same implicit reason why a child with EBD should be physically handicapped or suffer severe learning difficulties in the way that a child with such handicaps might suffer from EBD. The concept of EBD approaches closely that of 'not fitting in', which in turn approaches closely that of 'having a special educational need'. The EBD category has a conglomerate rag-bag quality to it and it is not surprising that the writers of the Special Educational Needs Report should have noted that children with EBD 'have few common distinguishing features'.

In fact, this issue of 'not fitting in' or of being 'maladjusted' to one's surrounds (and perhaps to oneself) is the nub of EBD. The issue figures prominently in the paragraphs describing the EBD group in the Special Educational Needs Report. The term 'adjustment' or 'maladjustment' crops up some nine times in the space of those five paragraphs. Reference is made to the aetiology of maladjustment, its underlying problems, to more work being required in assessing the needs of different subgroups within the maladjusted group, and to the re-issuing of an earlier HMSO pamphlet on 'The Education of Maladjusted Children'. It is noted that the term 'maladjusted' implies that behaviour can sometimes be most usefully read only in relation to the circumstances in which it occurs. As such the term is seen as a serviceable description and in the view of the writers of the Report should be retained alongside the term EBD (see para. 3.27). Certainly, from the Special Educational Needs Report, it may reasonably be concluded that the categories

2

of EBD and maladjusted children closely overlap. In what follows, little attempt will be made to distinguish between EBD and Maladjustment.

EBD MALADJUSTMENT: A SOCIAL JUDGEMENT

At the back of both the terms EBD and maladjustment, the conventional model assumes a central nuclear norm from which may be derived a number of deviations. The nuclear norm covers behaviour which a controlling group ('society') expects to be done, the 'desirable' way of doing things. The deviations cover behaviour which falls outside this expected, desirable pattern. EBD or maladjusted behaviour lies at the more undesirable end of the deviant scale.[6]

Implicit in the model, then, is the assumption of one group of people ('society', 'the school', 'the family') judging another in terms of the judger's ethos. The ultimate background to the idea of maladjustment is the evolution of rules and the corresponding emergence of a social group.[7] This background includes such questions as: (shifting) norms and deviations; (desirable) social change and the (permissible) means of bringing this about; the effectiveness and constraints on agencies appointed by society for bringing about and maintaining such social change; the progress and suppression of rebellion (freedom fighters and terrorists).

The imposition of rules creates conformers and rebels. Very soon in the study of maladjusted children we become aware of two phenomena which reflect the results of rules: polarization and scapegoating.

Case 1:[8] Craig and James were two brothers separated by a gap of two and a half years. Craig, the elder, always seemed older and larger than his years. With a restless, roving spirit he was the one who was always in trouble. His presence antagonized his father from the start, coming as it did between husband and wife. Craig's mother had a soft spot for him since her childhood too was marked by 'maladjustment'. (She attended Special Schools for the Maladjusted from 9 years on). James in contrast was the quiet studious second son whose conscientious efforts won him constant success and popularity. James was his father's favourite. But though she was proud of him, there were times when his mother resented James's good fortune: just too good to be true.

Craig for most of the time found his younger brother hard to stomach and would often try and get him into trouble. These efforts always misfired and Craig would sink deeper into the circle of punishments and further misdoings. In one important sense, as his mother perceived, Craig acted as the whipping boy for James and spared him not only the experience of doing wrong and getting punished but also the need to explore worlds where one took risks and sometimes failed.

This case illustrates a not uncommon story in families whereby one member becomes selected as 'the good one', the child who obeys the rules, and another as 'the bad one', the one who is always in trouble for testing the limits and disobeying the rules. The family becomes polarized around these two children and the family functions on this system of polarization.

A related way of functioning is by the (unconscious) selection of a scape-goat.

Case 2: 'If it wasn't for her we'd have had a lovely holiday. But she always manages to spoil it for us.' Tracey's parents seemed perfectly suited to each other. They were not only the same shape (short and fat); they seemed to think the same thoughts at the same time. At any rate they spent most conversations with themselves or others agreeing with each other, confirming sometimes in identical words what the other had just said. In this and other ways, they moved through life like some contented hermaphrodite, the perfect two in one. The only trouble was the air of somnolence they spread around them. Tracey was rising seven, and decided she did not want to go to sleep for the rest of her life. Worse still for her, she decided to wake her parents up.

Case 3: Tom's parents kept a spotless house where, as he told his friend Jim (with apparent pride), even the toilet is carpeted. His parents had been brought up with very clear ideas about cleanliness and hygiene. Being clean ('in body and mind') was desirable, good, and healthy. Being dirty was undesirable, bad, and sick. People appreciated you if you were clean. They did not want to know you if you were dirty. So you naturally made every effort to present a clean face to the world and to hide the other end of yourself, which had to do with sex and excretion, as though it did not exist. Unmentionable. These attitudes which his parents

4

held in common were what had brought and welded them together. These and their work as Court Ushers. The attitudes and
the work played a significant part in prompting Tom to respond
by what his parents called at different times his maladjustment,
sickness, or plain God-damned wickedness. Tom's immediate
responses took two forms: soiling and stealing. His less immediate
responses were guilt and confusion.

Tracey challenged the Sleepy System. She refused to be anaesthet-
ized. Tom too was caught in a similar childhood dilemma: do I
please my parents and comply with their demands; or do I try to
shake them out of their habitual (stultifying) ways?

Was Tom adjusted or maladjusted? The decision rests on your
vantage point. If the parents' ethic is accepted, with its clear separation of clean/good/healthy from dirty/bad/sick, then his parents
were right in deeming Tom maladjusted. He was rebelling against
being socialized along the lines they had defined. If, on the other
hand, the ethic is not accepted, then his behaviour must be read as
an early attempt towards a healthier adjustment for himself and
his parents. He is cast as the Reformer who resists an arbitrary
polarization and discrimination. He seeks to embrace what has
become the shadow in the family experience. He points a new way
ahead.

In setting EBD or maladjustment in perspective, the first question
we have to ask is: adjusted/maladjusted to what? For Tom and
others like him, this means not just asking why he is not fitting in
but what he is being expected to fit into. EBD or maladjusted
behaviour cannot be assessed in isolation from the context in which
it occurs. This context is littered with value judgements stemming
from religious, political, and economic influences, from childhood
rearing patterns across generations, from stereotypes, psychological
(mis)perceptions, and so on.

Moreover, for children in the flux of development, the context for
the assessment is not a point of time, a photograph, but a film in
space-time. It is not just a question of a child failing to fit into his
or her class today, but of fitting in today but not yesterday or
tomorrow. It is a question of 'catching up' or 'growing up' so that
a different child fits in tomorrow from the one that fails to fit in
today. Or of the class (or teacher) changing to accommodate to this

same child or reject him. Embedded in the term (mal)adjustment in childhood are diachronic as well as synchronic relations.[9]

ADJUSTMENT/MALADJUSTMENT: CONTRARIETY[10] AND CONTINUITY

In the conventional model of maladjustment we find a clearly marked division between adjusted and maladjusted behaviour. Adjusted behaviour is what the group approves of and finds desirable, while maladjusted behaviour is what it finds undesirable. We have already noticed some difficulties over clearly distinguishing between adjustment and maladjustment and over equating the desirable (socially approved) with adjusted and the undesirable (socially disapproved) with maladjusted behaviour.

Here I would like to press the examination a step further by starting from a well-established though often questionable practice: namely, the tendency to use one side of a distinction to define the other in a circle of reciprocity. We know what behaviour is in the pale by defining what behaviour lies beyond it, and vice versa. Maladjusted is the inverse of adjusted behaviour and adjusted the inverse of maladjusted.

This reading of one side as the inverse of the other is logically watertight if the relation between the two sides is that of a contradiction, i.e. if B is strictly not-A. In Tom's case, above, if dirty is strictly not-clean, and not-clean is strictly not-desirable, and not-desirable is strictly not-adjusted, then Tom's behaviour would be correctly read as maladjusted. But are any of these contradictions valid? May there not be some dirty actions which turn out to be clean, and desirable? May there not be some actions undesirable to some but quite desirable and hence adjusted to others?

In addition to our first question, 'adjusted or maladjusted to what?', we now have to add a rider, 'and under what circumstances?'. For even on a cursory investigation, adjustment is found not to be the strict opposite of maladjustment. The relation between the two is not that of contradiction but that of contrariety. For there is often an area of overlap where a piece of behaviour may be read by different persons or even the same person as either adjusted or maladjusted. There are occasions when 'adjusted' behaviour may not at the time (let alone later) be necessarily seen as desirable, good, or healthy, nor 'maladjusted' behaviour as necessarily EBD, undesirable, bad, or sick.

Case 4: Catharine, aged nine, was an obedient child brought up in the Catholic faith. Amongst other rules she learnt that you should always love, honour, and obey your parents and do what they asked of you. When her mother, who was not a Catholic, left her father, who was, and who managed to get his first marriage annulled and take a second wife, Catharine found herself in a triangular whirpool. And in trying to love, honour, and obey each parent in turn, her father, her ex-mother, and her new stepmother, each with their very different demands and viewpoints, she became quite confused and torn apart. In seeking to comply (to adjust to demands) she became maladjusted, becoming increasingly distractible in her school work and leisure hours.

Catharine's case is not an isolated one. Winnicott drew a valuable distinction between True and False Selves[11]. For Catharine, her False Self was the socially hyper-attuned one and her apparently adjusted behaviour turns out to be crippling. The generic features of 'adjustment' include such ambiguous qualities as conformity and compliance, and any attempt to assess Catharine's behaviour and its inverse in terms of the adjusted and maladjusted divide must run into major difficulties precisely because of the ambiguities in some of these generic qualities.

The generic features of 'maladjustment' similarly include such equally ambiguous qualities as change and rebellion (cf. Cohen on the generic features of the verb 'to deviate': alter course; stray; depart from; wander; digress; twist; drift; go astray; change; revolutionize; diversify; dodge; step aside).[12]

Case 5: 'When I was pregnant with him, I always wanted him to be a bit of a Denis the Menace', confessed a single parent of her only child, and goes on to recall her own over-conforming childhood. Paradoxically she brought this only child for 'treatment' of the subversive (maladjusted) behaviour which she had always envied in him.

It goes without saying that the 'treatment' never got off the ground; for however else one reads this mother's presentation of her child for treatment, one matter is certain: she was certainly not subscribing to the idea that all maladjusted behaviour is necessarily undesirable, bad, or sick. Such ambiguous signals on the part of the group defining what it deems to be desirable behaviour introduce for the child confusions that in themselves prompt a degree of maladjustment, though of a different order.

Pursuing the analysis, then, this divide between adjustment and maladjustment comes to resemble a continuous line rather than a step or a break between the polarities. Frequently, in the middle of a tirade about their child's 'impossible carry-on', a parent will suddenly relent and change tack. Each undesirable maladjusted act will be matched by a correspondingly endearing and ultra-adjusted one. When confronted by these parental volte-faces, the experience is of being swung vertiginously between one extreme of maladjusted and the other of adjusted behaviour across distinguishing cut-off points that are as arbitrary as they are elusive.[13]

THE PROTEAN FORM OF EBD MALADJUSTMENT

Partly because of the contrariety and continuity in the relation between maladjustment and adjustment, partly because there are few areas of human behaviour which are immune to some measure of adjustment/maladjustment, the presenting forms that any piece of EBD or maladjusted behaviour may take are varied and changing.

To the previous two questions, 'Maladjusted to what?' and 'Under what conditions?', we would now add a third: 'Assuming what form?'.

Here we are caught up in social swings and roundabouts already touched upon at the beginning of this chapter. A central principle in the 1944 Education Act was that every child should be educated in accordance with his or her age, ability, and aptitude. An extension of this principle was that special facilities had to be set up to cater for the variations that exist in these three characteristics. Special categories of facilities for special categories of handicaps were established. A child with impaired hearing would find him- or herself in a special school for the deaf; a partially sighted child in a special school for the partially sighted; and a child 'ascertained' as maladjusted (i.e. in the words of the Handicapped Pupils and School Health Regulations of 1945, showing signs of 'educational instability or psychological disturbance' requiring special educational treatment in order to effect his or her 'personal, social or educational readjustment') would most likely find him- or herself bound for a special school for the maladjusted.

The connection between this categorization/segregation and subsequent (educational) career, including the possibility of a career in deviancy, was duly noted.[14] By the end of the 1960s, the groundswell of educational opinion was changing. One of the main themes in the Special Educational Needs Report (paras. 3.21–3.25) was the reduction of segregation and the abolition of statutory categorization.[15] Thus, a child who in the 1950s would have gone to a residential school for the maladjusted would now, in the 1980s, be much more likely to find him- or herself in a remedial class in a mainstream school, or in a local day-unit. 'Dyslexia' and 'Learning difficulties' along with modification programmes came to the fore, though it was not always appreciated how closely these groups might overlap with EBD.

Case 6: Tom's father walked out on the family when the boy was 4 and just starting to read, an activity he loved his father to help him with. The father's departure, though the culmination of several years of marital bickering, nonetheless came as a shock to his wife, who went around saying to everyone in earshot: 'How am I going to cope?' Inevitably her anxiety was communicated to the two children (Tom's sister was 2 years younger than him), compounded as it was in Tom's mind by the logical question: 'If Dad can do it, why not Mum also?', as well as by a genuine sense of loss and betrayal.

Tom was preoccupied with ideas that the family was going to break up. He found it hard to settle to any activity, let alone one that entailed concentrating on odd shapes and sounds called letters which he closely associated with his father's help. Over the mastering of these intellectual mysteries, he now harboured very mixed feelings and as soon as he sat down to read, his mind became even more confused than usual. The shapes grew ever more jumbled and muddled; he did not know whether he was going forwards or backwards, stepping into his father's shoes or reverting to the security of infancy. Some of this uncertainty in orientation and direction was apparent in his handling of syllables and words. God often popped out as Dog, male as lame.

A year later, Tom went to a private school, where they quickly insisted that he stop the nonsense and settle to his letters (how else could they justify the fees his father was grudgingly paying?). By now, however, Tom's learning troubles were well entrenched. They had become a constant source of battles with his mother in the evenings, his father at alternate weekends, and of course with his teachers. He left his private school in disgrace.

By 7, Tom was being processed through the forms and assessments which went with the Special Educational Needs panel. As a result of this process, he went first to a Special Remedial class and then, when this was not a sufficient resource to meet his needs, was moved to a Special School for Children with Learning Problems. His behaviour here continued to cause concern (though exactly whose was left somewhat open since it was not deemed specifically 'educational').

By 10, Tom was on the books of the Juvenile Bureau (a branch of the Police) for a number of minor delinquencies.

More recently, in another shift of emphasis, the spotlight has been focused on problems of the physical (particularly sexual) abuse of children. Again the overlap with EBD is apparent.

Case 7: Sylvie was the eldest child in a family of four, each by different fathers who never stayed around to see their children grow up. When she was 10, her mother, Pauline, was still only 25 and constantly at loggerheads with her own mother. From early on, Pauline and Sylvie were more like sisters than mother and daughter. They shared intimacies, including sexual confidences, and then would suddenly regret doing so and try to deny they had ever been close.

The first time things came to a head with Sylvie was when she was 7, and Herb, her mother's current boy-friend, 'interfered' with her. Exactly what happened between the two was never cleared up. All Pauline knew was that she came home one evening to find Herb fondling Sylvie without her knickers on and when she talked with her daughter afterwards it seemed this was not the first time it had happened.

In Pauline's eyes, this incident marked the start of Sylvie's becoming maladjusted and beyond her control. She was not surprised when two years later, something similar happened with Sylvie and Peter, a mentally retarded 18 year old who was charged and found guilty.

By the time Sylvie was 13, she had sampled three secondary

schools, was well known to a wide network of agencies in the Health, Education, and Social Services, and was making regular appearances in the local Courts for increasingly serious brushes with the law.

As she grows up, Sylvie and those like her are turning to revenge. Reports of parents killed by the children they abused some years earlier are growing in number. Such reports are the extreme instances of widely ranging EBD, resulting from deep changes in family life and parenting (of which sexual abuse is only one aspect).

EBD or maladjusted behaviour reveals itself in a wide variety of forms with circular negative feedback often playing a major part in its emergence. This circle of feedback has long been known to involve other types of handicap (learning/physical, or the seering affront of sexual abuse). The child who finds reading difficult becomes an object of amusement in class and his or her response is to assume the role of buffoon or delinquent. The child with a 'mild' physical handicap becomes caught up in similar circles of derision and humiliation, leading to conduct disorder. Equally, the circle may start from a socio-psychological base and lead to physical damage. The child whose distractibility renders impossible his or her settling to read or whose depression and sense of failure becomes overwhelming gets caught up in an 'accident' (literally run over, or self-starvation, or rape, or an illness such as asthma or ulceration of the gut). This 'accident' in turn translates events in the circle into another orbit.[16]

In keeping EBD or maladjusted behaviour in perspective, we have to be aware not only of these many forms and circles that shape the behaviour, but also of an inevitable tendency to label different features of these long-recognized aetiological patterns in different ways and different times. Equally inevitable, then, is the fact that such labels and labelling are bound to shape our overall appreciation of the problem and our decisions on the optimal distribution of services for dealing with it.

IDENTIFICATION OF EBD OR MALADJUSTMENT: THE PARADOX OF PLANNING

Planning and its corollary, classifying, puts the planner for EBD on the horns of a dilemma (see Special Educational Needs Report, para. 3.30). The advantage of defining, for local education authorities and others, a series of established needs under clear cognomens, and of ensuring that a band of experts is at hand to cater for the problems that each cognominal group throws up, has to be balanced against some clear disadvantages, entailing the return of 'separateness' by the backdoor.[17]

For the agents whom society appoints as experts can so easily slip unawares into amplifying that very maladjusted behaviour on which their job depends, institutionalizing and consolidating the very category which their service is designed to resolve.

Again there is the effect of the system on those deemed EBD or maladjusted.

> **Case 8**: Hector, the youngest of seven, was by nature a dreamer. Before he reached school, he had flown around the globe in Superman's shoes, carrying out heroic rescues and finding it as exciting to be on the side of the rescued as on that of the rescuer, of the bad as on that of the good. In the early days at school, he used the same tactic as he found had worked at home: the unnoticed corner with the comic, and the occasional act of devastation, the originator of which went undetected. Hector enjoyed acts of devastation and he enjoyed even more escaping from them scot-free. When the finger of suspicion was finally pointed at him, and he was labelled and sent to a Special School as suffering from EBD, he interpreted this move as giving him unbridled licence to disrupt. 'How can I be expected to behave? I'm emotionally disordered. I'm maladjusted.' Any attempts on the part of the school to modify this attitude were resisted as being grossly 'unfair'. (The school was known in the neighbourhood as the one for the emotionally disordered and maladjusted – less politely as the Maladjusted Nutty School for Nutters).

We need groups and labels to plan. Yet saddled with this label, a child's past tends to be re-interpreted by him- or herself and others in the light of it. The child's future tends to be fashioned in the light of this re-interpretation.[18]

What guide-lines can be suggested to counter this planner's dilemma? In the first place, it would seem essential to submit regularly any piece of EBD/maladjusted behaviour to the three questions noted earlier: 'Maladjusted to what?', 'Under what conditions?', and 'Taking what form?'.

Any such submission must serve to place the piece of behaviour in a wider and (hopefully) more balanced perspective, for under these questions, the debate shifts immediately from the exposed individual to the context in which he or she is living. The EBD or maladjusted gesture becomes interpreted not only in terms of the individuals and those immediately about them but in terms of the social groups, the culture of which they are a part. The investigation becomes an exercise in mini-ethnography. In taking time out to explore the child's 'world view', others involved with him or her may find their own views expanding since the exercise is bound to bring into question previously unacknowledged stereotypes and other assumptions that are taken for granted.

The regular submissions will need to be undertaken at home and at school, and if a child is changing to a special unit or special school, before, during, and after this change. Again, within any special unit, the submissions will have to take account of the prevailing ethos in the unit, the tensions generated among staff who are daily dealing with EBD/maladjustment, and the relative isolation in which they are often obliged to work. (All these points will be taken up in greater detail in later chapters.)

Any piece of maladjusted behaviour may represent a paradox: sometimes adjusted and maladjusted for the same person at the same time; often adjusted and maladjusted for different people at different times. These paradoxes are often muddling, elusive, and hard to face. Yet it is essential to do so, holding on to them without attempting any facile and premature resolution.[19]

The regular submission inescapably will turn those involved (child, parents, and staff alike) inwards to consider their own sympathies or fury with a piece of EBD or maladjusted behaviour. For change to occur, people have to become aware of a personal dimension in the debate, of their own authentic feelings, and of the effect these feelings are having on their own EBD. In psychotherapy, such awareness is called countertransference and it is recognized as one of the most powerful means the therapist has for reaching out towards the nub of any situation. There is no reason why its use has to be confined to psychotherapy.

The language 'game' will then have to be played on a somewhat different base from that which is designed for administrative planning and which was referred to at the beginning of this chapter. However, the acceptance and analysis of these language differences offer us the best chance of living with planning paradoxes and of coming to grips with the experiential paradoxes of children in trouble and our efforts to be of any use to them.

NOTES

1 *Special Educational Needs. Report of the Committee of Enquiry into the Education of Handicapped Children and Young People* (Chairman: Mrs H. M. Warnock), London: HMSO, 1978.

2 L. Wittgenstein, *Philosophical Investigations*, Blackwell: Oxford, 1967.

3 See, for example, *The Report of the Underwood Committee on Maladjusted Children*, London: HMSO, 1955. See also Ministry of Education Circular 347 ('Child Guidance', March 1959) and 348 ('Special Educational Treatment for Maladjusted Children', March 1959).

4 The literature is extensive, but see initially B. Russell, *The Analysis of Mind*, Unwin, 1921, Chapters 3 and 14; G. Ryle, *The Concept of Mind*, London: Hutchinson, 1949, Chapter 4; I. Matte Blanco, *The Unconscious as Infinite Sets: An Essay in Bi-Logic*, London: Duckworth, 1975, Part 6; and M. Merleau-Ponty, *The Structure of Behaviour*, London: Methuen, 1965.

5 Again a wide field to choose from, but see initially William James's *Psychology, Vol. 2* for one side of the controversy, and the writings of the depth psychologists for the other side.

6 The conventional model is analogous to the statistical model of the Gaussian curve where the norm is located in the central part of the hump and deviations in the tails on either side. This curve has been found of great use in many fields where finite measurements and Aristotelian logic obtain. (See further in Matte Blanco, op. cit.) Outside the limits of such measurements and logic, the imposition of the Gaussian model may cloud rather than clarify our experience. In what follows it will be apparent that many aspects of 'maladjustment', especially in children, lie outside the limits of any simple Gaussian measures.

7 See M. Fortes, 'Rules and the Emergence of Society', *Occasional Papers of the Royal Anthropological Institute*, no. 39, 1983.

8 To preserve confidentiality, details in the case studies presented throughout this chapter have been changed and in this sense fictionalized. The points they exemplify are however all based on fact.

9 The significance of context for assessing mode and degree of (mal)adjustment takes us far beyond the confines of this chapter. Consider for a moment what adjustment means for a child brought up in the Falls Road in Belfast, or in the Lebanon, Basra, Kabul, Mozambique, Ethiopia, Nicaragua, and so on. Or the implications for 'maladjustment' among children from excessively poor or excessively rich families or on children denied childhood (see M. Winn, *Children without Childhood*, Harmondsworth: Penguin, 1984). The theme has fascinated novelists and film-makers: who are the well adjusted in

prison (*King Rat*), the Nazi Party (*Mephisto*), a mental hospital (*One Flew Over the Cuckoo's Nest*), a US naval College (*End of a Man*), a US rich family (*Rebel Without a Cause*), or an English public school (*If*).

10 For those not acquainted with the jargon of formal logic, contrariety is a relation distinguished from contradiction. In the relation of contradiction, two statements cannot both be true and cannot both be false. In the relation of contrariety, on the other hand, two statements can both be false though they cannot both be true. The relation of the statements 'Smith is a graduate' and 'Smith is an undergraduate' is that of contrariety since Smith could be one or the other or neither. Similarly, the relation of the statements 'Smith is adjusted' and 'Smith is maladjusted' is that of contrariety since (from the same or different viewpoints) Smith could be one or the other or neither.

11 See D. W. Winnicott, *The Family and Individual Development*, London: Tavistock, 1965, pp. 17–19 and 153.

12 See S. Cohen, (ed.), *Images of Deviance*, Harmondsworth: Penguin, 1971.

13 Some of the effects of this bi-polar spectrum model for adjustment/maladjustment, with its continuous line linking the two poles, may be found in related distinctions that are often used in filling out the reasons for maladjusted behaviour. One such distinction is that drawn between a physiological and psychological basis for the behaviour. The child acts in a particular way because he or she is physically handicapped, suffers from epilepsy, brain damage, or some other neurological condition; or at a more controversial level, because the child is dyslexic, autistic, or endogenously depressed.

A second distinction, in part an extension of the first, is that drawn between inner and outer (environmental) events. The child behaves this way because he or she is that sort of person, shaped along these lines not merely by physiology but by genetic inheritance and disposition (an introverted character).

Though of some value in providing headings for an assessment of maladjusted behaviour, these distinctions are in no way watertight. They may offer a multidimensional view into the setiology of maladjusted behaviour and some proportionate weighting for the various dimensions. But between one polar instance (such as brain damage or autism) where a high weighting may be given to physiological or inner change, and another (such as sexual abuse) where a high weighting may be given to socio-psychological events, lie the vast majority of cases where events from both poles contribute to the resultant behaviour, where the weightings tend to cancel each other out.

Often, the more we come to understand instances apparently at one polar extreme, the more we become aware of influences from the opposite pole.

14 See R. Higgins, 'The concept of maladjustment: its social consequences', *Human Relations* 16 (1963): 61.

15

15 In the UK, the movement away from segregated Special Schools, especially when residential, received support from an economic climate of increasing stringency and retrenchment. By the late 1970s, Local Educational Authorities were looking much more parsimoniously at the financing of ever more expensive placements in Special Schools, often residential and independently run.

16 See the many examples of circular patterns in various accounts of 'psychosomatic' illness. Also, for circularity in reading difficulties, see M. Rutter and L. A. Hersov, *Child Psychiatry: Modern Approaches*, Oxford: Blackwell Scientific Publications, 1977, p. 572.

17 The planning of appropriate services has been one of the main reasons advanced in the past for the fashioning of some sort of index of maladjustment, that is of some measure which will provide the planners with an indication of how prevalent or how serious maladjusted behaviour is at any time in the community. How many children should we estimate are EBD or 'maladjusted' both at present and as likely to become so in the future?

Such an Index tends to focus on individual behaviour and be derived from a summation of scores on a variety of scales, with the score above a certain level being defined arbitrarily as the cut-off point for unacceptable behaviour. See, for example, M. Rutter, J. Tizard, and K. Whitmore, *Education, Health and Behaviour*, London: Longman, 1970. (In fairness to these authors, it should be stressed that they are clearly not unaware of some of the snags inherent in the production of an index of maladjustment. See pages 150 and 179 of their book and also their preparation of separate forms (and so separate viewpoints) for parents, teachers, and doctors.)

The approach has analogies with studies in criminology that attempt to measure recidivism and is subject to the same arguments for and against. See T. Szasz, *Ideology and Insanity*, Harmondsworth: Penguin, 1974, Chapter 10.

The search for an index is likely to run into difficulties with those very aspects of EBD and maladjusted behaviour which have been explored in this chapter: the central significance of social context; the characteristic of contrariety/continuity in adjustment/ maladjustment behaviour patterns; and the Protean forms that EBD and maladjusted behaviour can assume. What emerges under the category of EBD or maladjusted behaviour in the index seems bound to be a summary picture foreshortened and distorted in the interest of political and statistical convenience.

18 See Szasz, T. op. cit. See also E. Goffman, *Asylums*, Harmondsworth: Pelican, 1968, and his *Stigma*, Harmondsworth: Pelican, 1968.

19 The paradoxes stem directly from the contrariety already noted in the adjustment/maladjustment relation. They touch on some central issues of our time: a naïve faith in planning and how to resist this; conscious/ unconscious awareness and different logics; the persistent relevance in our midst of 'the primitive mind'. See Matte Blanco, op. cit. See also M. Arden, 'Infinite sets and double binds', *International Journal of*

Psychoanalysis, 65 (1984): 443; M. Arden, 'Psychoanalysis and survival', *International Journal of Psychoanalysis* 66 (1985): 471; and T. M. S. Evens, 'Mind, logic and the efficacy of the Nuer incest prohibition', *Man* 18 (1983): 111.

Chapter Two

THE PSYCHODYNAMIC THEORY OF CHILDREN WITH EMOTIONAL AND BEHAVIOURAL DIFFICULTIES

CHRISTOPHER DARE

This chapter will demonstrate some psychoanalytic perspectives on children in distress, with little reference to treatment. The psychoanalytic understanding of people mostly comes from the treatment of adults and children, although direct observation of babies and children outside therapy is also adding to the store of psychoanalytic knowledge. Because of this derivation from psychotherapy;

> It follows that psychoanalytic views on the nature and course of psychological development are essentially generalizations perceived while looking back on the past. In treatment the analyst attempts to help the patient make sense out of his present life, symptoms, character traits, difficulties and interpersonal conflicts, in terms of past experiences. All aspects of psychoanalysis constitute a post dictive system.[1]

This aspect of psychoanalysis, its contribution to 'making sense of experience', is of great value for workers with emotionally and behaviourally disturbed children even where no type of psychoanalytic treatment is available in a formal way. The psychoanalytic provision of a detailed perception of what is going on supports the empathic skills of the adults responsible for the care and succour of children. The psychoanalytic stance of putting high priority on gaining awareness of subjective experience of the child gives professional activities an informed sympathy and humanity.

The chapter centres upon a case history of a child, the details of which have been altered to preserve confidentiality. Psychoanalytic concepts, as they contribute to the understanding of psychological difficulties, will be drawn upon after the exposition of the case history.

Any presentation of a case expresses a theoretical slant guiding the selection and organization of the material. As far as possible, however, the case is described in a straightforward way, emphasizing the child's point of view. Then, there comes a psychodynamic exposition beginning with classical psychoanalytic ideas especially in so far as they remain valid. Subsequently, post-Freudian concepts are introduced. Along the way, some general comments are made to facilitate generalization from the particular case.

A CASE HISTORY

Susan was 14, and for 5 years her father had sexually abused her. At first, when she was little, he held her on his lap more fiercely and too long for her to have felt quite comfortable. His kisses in bed on Sunday mornings had been 'sloppy' and she had not really liked them. She had been his favourite and her sister, Andretta, had always been 'mummy's pet'. When Susan's breasts had grown, her father had been very interested and kept 'checking that they were alright'. This involved her undressing when no one else was present. One day, however, he had started stroking and kissing her breasts and later still he began to have intercourse with her. To her surprise, she had not been surprised. When he first had undressed her and lain on top of her, it seemed quite horrible and disgusting and frightening, but not surprising. That puzzled her. It was so horrible, made her feel so crushed and shocked and awful and she hated being wet afterwards.

She had felt that the worst thing in the world would be that anyone else would know, but one day when she was 13½ and Mummy and Andretta were out shopping, Mum came back to get her cheque book and found Dad on top of Susan in the parents' bedroom. Susan had immediately felt that it was awful, that her mother would never forgive her but at least 'it' would stop. Her mother simply turned away! It was never talked about, and her father went on making her undress for him, and then he even made her kiss his 'thing', and he wet her inside her mouth. She thought that she was choking to death. She had felt sick and for several days had vomited after food. She got hold of the idea that dad did 'it' to her because he had gone off her mother for having put on so much weight. Susan had overheard her mother and father in a fierce quarrel. Mother had reproached her husband for giving more attention to Susan than to her and he had said: 'What do you expect, you have become a ******* fat cow.' Susan began quite deliberately to overeat to get fat. She had always been proud that she was slimmer than most girls in her class, when, at the same time her Uncle Brian and Aunt May had said that she had a 'beautiful little figure'. She thought that dad might stop doing 'it' if she got fat. She put on 3 stones in weight and dad told her off a lot for being greedy, but it did not stop him. If anything, he began to do 'it' more.

Since Mum had caught them he seemed to care less about when and where he made her undress. Sometimes Susan thought that he wanted to be seen: she had once opened her eyes when he was lying on top of her and had seen him looking in the mirror at their reflection. The more he seemed careless about being found out at home, the more he threatened her that he would kill her if she told anyone. She believed him. He had always been soft on her, but he had always had a frightening temper and hit her quite a lot in fury and she was terrified of his threats.

When the months had gone by, after mum had found them, and 'it' went on, Susan became more and more despairing and all the time day-dreamed about ways of getting her father to stop. Sometimes she thought of running away, but she had a horrible thought that he would then start doing 'it' to Andretta. Even though Susan felt less and less friends with Andretta, the thought of her father doing 'it' to Andretta was worse than having 'it' done to herself. Eventually, she thought that the only thing she could do was to spread a rumour about dad doing 'it' to her. She explained about her father having sex with her to one of her friends, Penny, at school, choosing her because Penny's mother, Mrs Peetle, was a teacher at the same school. She then plucked up even more courage to tell dad that someone at school had said that the window cleaner had seen him doing 'it' to her, 2 weeks ago. She told her dad that she had said that it was not true. The next day, at school, something strange happened. Mr Hills stopped her on the way to Design Technology. Mr Hills was a teacher who never seemed to teach anything, but sat in the 'Special Resource' and talked to some children on their own. He said he wanted to see her straight away. In his room he came to the point. He seemed nervous and did not look her in the eye. She had a sudden horrible idea that he was going to do as her father did. He said Mrs Peetle had been told by Penny that her father had been having intercourse with her. Was it true? She told him that she would never talk to Penny again for telling such lies. In her own mind she hoped that he would ask her parents to come to school and get them to punish her for telling lies, that it would frighten dad and that he would stop. Instead, Mr Hills said that he would see her the next day, and the next day and the next day, for as long as it would take for him to really know what was going on.

In the mean time he canvassed Susan's teachers. He found out that she was a clever, conscientious girl. People could not see her as Andretta's sister, because where Susan was serious and studious, quiet and imaginative, Andretta was sparkling and easy going, an actress, in her way, but nervous and easily tearful. Susan gave the impression that it was a matter of pride, for her, that no one would make her cry. For some time, Miss Fredericks, Susan's year teacher who also took Susan's class for English, had had an uneasy feeling that there was something wrong. She liked Susan, who she felt had a real feeling for poems about the country, unusual in the inner urban sophisticates in the third form. She felt that Susan shrank away from people and had an edge of misery and fear about her.

After 5 days, Mr Hills admitted he was baffled; he was sure that they could not forget about the rumour, and asked Miss Fredericks to try. With Miss Fredericks, in the English resources room, Susan admitted that her father had been cuddling her and touching her under her blouse and skirt, but she was adamant that nothing more had happened, that her dad loved her, that she loved him, and that they were a happy family. Miss Fredericks called the Social Services Department, and so a social worker and a WPC came to interview Susan, Andretta, and Mr and Mrs X, all separately. They all denied that there had ever been anything of any sort between Susan and her father other than the love and affection that was the hallmark of their family life. Susan felt relieved. The story was out, her dad would stop 'it'. Everything would go back to as it had been. To her horror, it was not so! The police decided there was no case against Mr X that would stand up in Court. The Social Services Department decided that there was too much likelihood of the rumour being true for Susan to go home. They took a Place of Safety Order removing Susan to a children's home.

Here, Susan's nightmare took a fresh turn. She had never seen such children. Her teachers prided themselves that they were up against the real problems of their inner urban geography, but it was not so. Susan's school was a former grammar school, and still retained a population of children from the largely stable middle-class ghetto around it. Not so the Children's Home. It drew its population from the high-rise, drug-ridden, desperate people of the borough's 1960s concrete architectural showplaces. In the Children's Home were the products of the socially disadvantaged and psychologically damaged. There, Susan found girls who, having been sexually abused by their fathers or stepfathers, had proudly turned to earning money for themselves and their boyfriends, 'uptown', as prostitutes. The favourite sport of these girls was attempting to discredit and dismiss staff of either sex, by seducing them. The boys were, Susan thought, mad. They were unpredictable, violent, and thieving, stupidly uninterested in school. They stole from her, swore constantly in the most vile way, and casually grabbed at her and fingered her. She immediately had to learn to scream and punch, to defend her body and her property. She was big and strong, in contrast to many of the other children, but she lacked their wild, desperate ruthlessness.

Susan became deeply depressed. She could think only of getting home. She was convinced that her father and mother would never forgive her for disgracing them, and indeed that was their attitude. They visited her rarely, saying it was her big mouth that had got her there, and it was her mouth that had to get her out. The Children's Home staff were deeply sorry for Susan. Her key worker had herself been sexually abused in her teens, by her half-brother. She talked for long hours to Susan about her own life and interests. Susan came to trust her, recognizing the residential worker's honesty, courage, and understanding. So Susan confided the truth, the escalating sexual passion of her father, her hopelessness, her plan to get 'it' stopped by spreading and denying the rumour.

With deep misgivings, the residential worker followed departmental instructions and filed a report. A field social worker interviewed Susan, who felt betrayed and horrified and said that it was all lies. Nothing had ever happened between her and her father. She loved him, loved her mother, and wanted to go home.

The school and the Social Services began to be irritated and frightened. The parents' solicitors not only believed the parents but had strong involvement in campaigns to protect parents' rights. The legal wrangles and professional heart-searching kept Susan in care, month after month. She told her social worker that she would kill herself if she was fostered. She began to accumulate street drugs, gained from itinerant inmates of the Children's Home. She was eating all the time, disgusted with her fatness and often vomiting to counteract the sense of guilt and anger with herself which she felt after her gross eating.

At school she was still hanging on academically and to her two friends with whom she could feel that some of her life was alright. She no longer trusted the teachers and was angry, surly, and moody with them. She told her friends of her suicidal plans and they told the teachers. Susan drew on her children's home language to discourage Mrs Frederick's tentative enquiry about her mood and intention. The school began to doubt Susan's veracity (though she had never been untruthful in the manner of some of their pupils).

The scandals, the bad language, and the outbursts against teachers began to disturb the staff room. The finale occurred in the playground. A loutish fourth former ran into Susan, pushed himself away, expressing crude admiration for her: 'lovely pair of buffers'. Susan drew a knife and cut his face. She was immediately suspended from the school and the Social Services Department was asked to find her another school.

At this stage, Susan was confused, angry, suicidal, with poor relationships with adults, professional and parental alike. She was moody, had shown poor impulse control, lacked self-esteem, and had a highly negative attitude to her gender identity. Her adolescent development was distorted, with a failure to integrate into peer and other role models and identifications. She thought a great deal about food, eating for the pleasure of having something in her mouth and for the comforting sense of fullness. After she had eaten, she thought, fleetingly, that she was repulsive and that was a gratifying punishment for her father. Following such a thought, she often found she had an image of her father's erect penis and huge bush of genital hair thrusting in her mouth. In some ways she would not reject the image because it made her vomit and got rid of some of the food she had just eaten.

She resorted to self-destructive fantasies to attempt to alleviate her unhappy mood. When she thought of killing herself, she imagined specifically that she would be transformed into a slim, girlish angel.

She thought of her father dying of guilt and grief, and imagined a vivid scene in heaven where she and her father met, embraced, he asked her forgiveness, and the reunion was completed.

Technically, at this stage, Susan could be said to be behaviourally and emotionally disturbed.

THE NATURE OF PSYCHOANALYSIS

Psychoanalysis is a rich and varied approach to the understanding of the human condition.[2] It consists of a number of theories of how the mind is formalized which share a number of basic assumptions.[3] The theories are sometimes in opposition to each other, but more often, they are complementary and integrate to give a wide-ranging and subtle understanding of the human personality. These theories comprise 'psychoanalytic psychology'. This is based not upon experimental methods of other academic psychologies but upon an intuitive understanding of people acquired during the vigorous and demanding practice of psychoanalysis (using the word as a description of psychoanalytic treatments). Because of this derivation, psychoanalytic psychology, in some ways, more resembles the intuitive or inspirational psychology of the sort displayed by poets and novelists than it does the treatises of experimentalists who can 'know' only that which has been 'proved' by the disciplines of academic research. By the same token it is a derivative of common-sense psychology that we use all the time for the conduct of personal relationships, business, and customary social manipulations.

However, there are difficulties that arise in any account of psychoanalytic propositions because of the dual meaning of the word and the long history of the subject. Discussions about the scientific status and practice of psychanalysis often demonstrate confusion.

The word psychoanalysis has two broad meanings, the one usage describing a psychology (cf. Sandler et al. 1973[4]) and the other that of a clinical practice, a dominant and diverse psychotherapy. In addition to the confusion that comes from the dual meaning of the word there are complexities that derive from the historical and geographical development of psychoanalysis. Over nearly a century psychoanalysis both as a general psychology and a clinical practice has changed in innumerable ways.[5]

To take account of these difficulties, this chapter will adopt a some-what historical approach, beginning by stating what can be derived from Freud himself, to understand children in difficulties, and then summarizing later contributors. The intention is not to give a full and scholarly account of the development of psychoanalytic thinking about children in distress. The emphasis will be upon those aspects of the psychoanalytic models that seem to the present author to have a continuing usefulness for those engaged in helping disturbed children and adolescents.

FREUD'S CONTRIBUTION

It is striking that Freud never worked directly with children, and there was no tradition amongst his professional contemporaries of giving psychotherapeutic help to children. Despite this, one of Freud's most original and important contributions to psychology has been to place the experience of childhood as being of crucial importance to the development of the adult personality. In particu-lar, Freud showed that it was possible to make direct connections between childhood happenings and adult states.

Freud, throughout his long and evolving career, always proceeded from detailed observation of a particular condition towards more general propositions about psychological processes. The time at which he had begun his career coincided with the contemporane-ously ever spreading network of the European railways system, and inevitably, accidents happened. Neurologists and other doctors found themselves presented with victims of such accidents, whose experiences produced mental rather than physical consequences. The conditions were thought to be allied to hysterical phenomena, as then understood.

It is not surprising, therefore, that the first clinical theories that Freud espoused emphasized the 'traumatic neuroses' as the model of all psychological disturbances.[6] The form of his model was shaped by the clinical context that he offered to his patients. This context showed Freud's great originality as a therapist: he offered people with manifestly psychological problems a threefold opportunity: first, his patiently intense attention; second, a non-judgemental priv-acy and confidentiality; and third, an assumption that what they went through and what they said were likely to make some sense. The purpose of the clinical context that Freud provided for his patients' was to enable him to disentangle the underlying 'meaning' of the presenting problem. This was not only of enormous therapeutic potential but it also had a humanistic, ethical quality, respecting the authenticity and the value of a person's experience. The psychoanalytic approach to children embodies the great ethical value of the tradition deriving from Freud's work, stressing that what children say and how they behave has a meaning. It continues to be vital to ensure that children's experiences are given full and sensitive adult attention. All too often, those who work with children have schedules or protocols that are directed towards the needs of children but which do not require that caretakers have the empathic and intuitive skills to find out a particular child's precise experiences and needs. Alternatively, those who work with children have a dedication to espousing the child's point of view but take what the child says as their only source for assessing the child. What children say in a particular context and at a particular stage of their development requires knowledgeable assessment as well as an absorbing sympathy.

Freud's age was one of relative but not absolute sexual puritanism and prudishness and perhaps it was a time when sexual expressiveness was difficult to achieve. Under such circumstances, it is possibly not surprising that many of Freud's patients, when encouraged to talk about their innermost thoughts, told him of the sexual events of their lives.

He developed the conviction that many adult disturbances arose in situations that resembled Susan's tragedy. In late nineteenth-century Vienna, however, parental authority and the taboo on revelation of sexual abuse were at a much higher level than in the present world. Susan would not have told anyone of her abuse, except in the unlikely prospect of having gained admission to Freud's consulting room. At this stage of Freud's career, he would have regarded Susan as having had an experience in childhood that had one sort of meaning, which, in adolescence and with greater sexual awareness, would have taken on different connotations. This was as it seems to have been with Susan. As a 9 year-old she was frightened and hurt by her father's sexual interest. She had some sense that it was prohibited, and his warnings to keep it secret backed up her own embarrassment and deep shame and guilt. When she had begun to be more emotionally and sexually mature, with puberty, Freud argued at this time, she would have reevaluated her abuse. Her understanding of its meaning and her knowledge of the forbidden nature would have been even more intense. She would also begin to be much more conscious of why her mother would be angry, hurt, and betrayed by the abuse. Freud showed that the adolescent would have to cope with the emotions aroused by her re-evaluation of the trauma. Furthermore, she would have to struggle to manage the emotions as they pressed for some form of discharge, accompanied by clear memories of her earlier and current experiences. Freud saw that the mind could be overwhelmed by the intense feelings, leading to certain symptoms. Susan's general irritability and misery would be one form of expression of the feelings. Her increasing certainty that she had to find a way to put a stop to it would be in accord with the notion of relentless and pressing feelings needing some form of discharge.

When she had told her story, in the only way that she felt she could, and it had not stopped her abuse, Susan became even more burdened by the realization that what had happened to her raised even more taboos than she had expected. She was appalled by her mother's failure to have acknowledged her need, siding, so it seemed, with her father. Susan developed a habit of eating a lot, to vomiting up her food, which, at this stage of Freud's theorizing, would have been thought to be a symbolic attempt to expel father's penis from her mouth and so purge herself of the alarming feelings and images.

The ideas of 'purging' the mind of overwhelming ideas and feelings are of ancient origin, but produced by Freud in his early theories, in the specific way outlined here, in accordance with the model of the mind as being designed to manage ideas and their attached affects. Treatment was considered to be largely 'cathartic', helping the person eliminate feelings and ideas that had been derived from traumatic experiences.

Catharsis remains an important ingredient of counselling and psychotherapy and certainly Susan would have been helped by the opportunity to reveal all her experiences. She needed to express the feelings that had been aroused in her, both those that were conscious and those that by their prohibited nature were kept from consciousness. Unfortunately, of course, Susan's fate after she had revealed the abuse made it difficult for her to confide her innermost thoughts to the many sympathetic adults whom she encountered.

After some years of working with patients, using a view of

psychological problems as being essentially traumatic in origin, Freud became aware of an increase of an inadequacy in the model. He became increasingly interested in the sexual development of children, as it was expressed in the course of the psychotherapy of adults. He also became more aware of the great complexity of emotional life, being especially impressed by and interested in those aspects of mental life that were vigorously kept out of consciousness. These interests were particularly stimulated by studies of the associations to dreams that he himself had had, or those that were related by patients in therapy.

Freud noted that which those who care for children can also see – that children are sexual beings. The nature of childhood sexuality is different from that of adults, but nonetheless it exists and presents a force to be managed within the child. Freud evolved a model of the mind that took account of the sequential stages in the development of children's sexuality.[7] The main feature of the model was that great importance was given to the wishes arising within the person that derived from aspects of their sexual instinctual drives. Some of these wishes were acceptable to consciousness, but some were not, and it was these that both stimulated the development of fantasy and play, but also had effects upon basic character organization.

In analysing sexual development Freud attended to those aspects of sexuality which in his time were thought of as abnormal or perverse. Nowadays it is more widely understood that the sexual response is a complex one and involves more than simple genital contact. However, the different feelings aroused by different aspects of sexuality are well represented in Susan. She had had a sensible sexual education that had provided her with information about the conception and development of the child. She knew 'the facts of life' about sexual intercourse.

She was completely unprepared, as any child, for the size of her father's penis and the extent of his pubic hair. She was quite unable to cope with his oral demands. Her reactions to these events were by conscious horror and disgust and an unconscious turning of the wish to reject into vomiting food.

There was another aspect of her sexual development that naturally was aroused by her experiences. She had been her father's favourite and he had been her favourite parent. This is something which is often observed with an older child. The younger child, having been born, interrupts a relatively exclusive closeness between the first child and mother. The elder child turns to father, who may, himself, feel excluded by his wife's preoccupation with the new baby.

As Susan grew up and appreciated her father's love and resources, she would naturally have become attached to him. In the pre-school years, as a perception of the workings of the world impinged upon her and as she imagined herself becoming adult, she would have come to expect that her future partner would be her father. The realization that her father and mother were also partners would come to be experienced as a complication.[8] Such feelings ('the Oedipus complex') are quite overt and conscious in pre-school children, but as time goes on they become manifestly socially unacceptable and are forcibly excluded from the conscious mind.

Behaviourally, Susan remained closely attached to her father and this did not waver despite his abuse of her. However, when he abused her, her unconscious memories and wishes for him as a husband were revived. Some of her distress and pain arose as a reaction to the fulfilment of unconscious wishes. The strongest consequences, however, were in the development of enormous guilt feelings that were so manifest and distressing. Such guilt feelings contributed to the muddle that she created during her efforts to protect herself and which rebounded upon her. Above all, her suicidal wishes can be seen as, in part, an expression of a guilt-driven self-punishment. In her fantasy, killing herself mainly eliminated her sexuality and enabled her to believe in a desexualized reunion with her father in heaven.

The belief that girls may have wishes to seduce their fathers is not confined to psychoanalysts. In dealing with the (male) lawyers and barristers involved in Susan's case, it was clear that they often inclined to the belief that she had invented her allegations. Even her schoolteachers, who had good reason to respect her probity, had occasional doubts. None of these professionals could put forward a sensible reason why Susan should make up such stories. The psychoanalytically sensitive observer would wonder if it was to do with the professionals' own unconscious knowledge of the power of Oedipal feelings that led them to such doubts about Susan's situation.

Another aspect of Susan's protectiveness to Andretta can be understood in terms of her unconscious wishes for exclusive possession of her father. Some of her abhorrence at the thought of her sister suffering the same fate as herself can be put down to a real altruism. Some of the intensity can be understood as a wish to be the only one to whom father was attracted, even though the attractions were so awful.

Later in the evolution of Freud's thinking, he refined his model of the mind to take more account of the factors which seemed to be operating in Susan as described in the last few paragraphs. He came to realize that the particular qualities and personality of a person were intimately responsive to the character of the parents they had lived with in their upbringing. Freud and later psychoanalysts have not completely rejected the effects of traumatic experiences on children. The idea of the accumulating impact of repeated trauma, qualitatively similar traumas, has been suggested as a more regular antecedent of emotional and behavioural disorder than a single massive trauma.[9] This concept is obviously very relevant to Susan and many other children in difficulties that we see. However, a further and perhaps more generally applicable notion is to think in terms of *traumatic relationships*[10] rather than traumatic incidents. This suggests that attention should be paid not only to the actual incidents that occur in a child's life and that may distort development and lead to problems, but also to the overall quality of the relationships experienced by the child. Of course there may be an immediate and obvious connection between what the child experiences and what would seem to be happening by an observer. At other times, what the child experiences is idiosyncratic, being the child's own interpretation, which has its own validity, but may not accord with what a knowledgeable observer would predict.

These persisting ideas on the importance of considering the traumatic qualities in a child's upbringing take us ahead of Freud's lifetime. In the first decade of this century he realized that many adults suffered, and in some ways impose suffering upon themselves, on account of strong but unconscious guilt. Many children in trouble do indeed have the powerful theme of self-punishment in their repeated entanglements with authority. Such children openly create uncertainty and anger in the minds of caring adults. Such a phenomenon was at work, inside and around Susan.

At other times, children can be seen to be conducting themselves in ways that do not conform with their own character or even their own needs. Some such behavioural and emotional states can be seen to be in keeping with ways of thinking and ideals which come from their parents or other important adults. Because of the prominence of ideals and conscience in shaping behaviour and personality, Freud suggests that there was a structure in the mind, the super-ego, that embodied significant demands, rules, prohibitions, and expectations. He pointed out that these have been internalized as the outcome of the relationship between the developing person and their parents.

Susan can be seen to be tormented by the wish, on the one hand, to comply with her parents' demand, to say that theirs was a normal, uncomplicated family, and on the other, her actual knowledge of the reality.

Freud came to suggest that there was a distinctive part of the mind, the ego, which represented the realities of the external world and which developed capabilities enabling a person to live according to the exigencies of the external world. Susan's pain and misery are understandable as being the outcome of the conflict between her wish to preserve herself, by the tenets of her own perceptions of reality, and that which her parents wanted her to say. The power of the latter was enhanced both by her love for her parents, but also by her emotional and physical dependence upon them.

Many disturbed children are in such conflict as Susan found herself. Those who work with them should try to understand the nature of the conflicts from which they suffer and for which they have to find necessarily compromising solutions.

At the same time that Freud adumbrated the notion of the ego, serving reality and the integration of the mind, and the super-ego, serving the internalized demands and ideals of the parents, he described the id. This was a part of the mind, Freud suggested, that housed the powerful, tumultuous, instinctual drives whose energies vitalized a person but whose aims had to be curbed both according to the demands of reality (the ego) and to that of society (through the agency of the super-ego). Just as there can be conflict between the ego and super-ego, so there can be between the id and the ego or the id and the super-ego. In so far as Susan had some wish to have an exclusive and (deeply repressed) sexual relationship with her father, there was a conflict of that aspect of her super-ego that was built upon her father's and her mother's rules. That is an id/ super-ego conflict as is often experienced by adolescents in mild turmoil as they feel that they are developing sexual wishes and are apparently disobeying parental rules.

At the same time, of course, her father would be likely to find himself breaking his own rules, in allowing himself a sexual relationship with his daughter. Freud pointed out that children are aware when parents break their own rules, and experience themselves something of the parents' own turmoil and conflict. Susan was especially troubled by her mother's denial of the facts, as they were known to her, of the father's sexual abuse of his daughter. When parents break rules that at the same time they enjoin children to obey, they create confusion in children. Some delinquent children seem to have a great deal of emotional upset that derives from such situations.[11]

Susan was especially troubled when as a result of her revelation she was placed in the care of the Local Authority. In the Children's Home she came up against children who were flagrant in their disregard of the rules of behaviour that Susan expected of herself. It added strongly to her sense of being seen as delinquent for having told of her father's abuse. It also emphasized the unfairness of what was happening to her. To the young person who is grappling with the acceptance of regulation for behaviour that goes against their wishes for instinctual gratification, unfairness, the realization that adults are not conforming to their own rules is poignant and bewildering.

So far, I have presented Freud's contribution to ways of understanding children with emotional and behavioural problems. Since his death in London in 1940, however, there has been an enormous amount of work carried out by psychoanalysts with children in distress. None of this work has negated the perception of Susan expressed thus far. I will summarize three major lines of development in psychoanalysis, continuing to use Susan as the example. During the last two decades of Freud's life, two women psychoanalysts were developing the discipline of psychoanalysis. One was Freud's daughter, Anna Freud.

THE CONTRIBUTION OF ANNA FREUD

Anna Freud developed her father's ideas and gave rise to a school of psychoanalysis that in the USA has been extremely influential, known as 'ego-psychology'. The approach stemmed from the intensive clinical work with children of Anna Freud.[12] Her contemporary and close colleague, Heinz Hartmann[13] worked mainly with adults in developing ego-psychology. As the name implies, ego-psychology focused upon the nature of the controlling and integrating capacities of the mind. These are divided into two: the ego apparatuses and the ego function. The former, the apparatuses, were considered to develop spontaneously as the innate givens of the person. They comprise the capacities of perception, of learning, of memory and control of motor skills, and of language and speech. Speech, learning, perception, memory, and motor control can be distorted by psychological conflicts but the overall capacities of the person are dependent upon intactness of these ego-apparatuses. Children can be profoundly affected by limitations of their innate endowment or from developmentally damaging injury (from illness or physical trauma). On the other hand, good endowments, being sound of limb, eye, and mind, can give the child resources to withstand disadvantages in other areas. No assessment of the child is complete unless the presence or absence of such factors are considered.

Strictly speaking, control of memories, speech, and so on are the function of the ego-apparatuses and hence of the ego. There is, however, a large range of ego functions that are not the outcome of the activities of the motor and perceptual systems but are more clearly specific to mental processes. These functions can be divided into a number of areas that are important for appreciating the processes of child psychology and the development of the personality. The first area is that of the *defence*. Freud had described various types of mental mechanisms whereby the mind coped with unacceptable ideas or feelings. Anna Freud refined and categorized these processes.

A number of defences can be seen operating in Susan's mind. Thus, for example, when her father began his abuse, for a while Susan seems not to have appreciated what was happening. She repressed her (albeit childish) knowledge of intercourse and achieved a state of mind whereby the significance of the experience was not acknowledged. Repression and denial are related. In the first, if total, all knowledge of a painful, overwhelming experience is eliminated from consciousness. Sometimes, Susan denied anything having taken place, and the attitude that she had was that there was no cause for concern. It was unclear as to whether this was simply a conscious strategy of denial or whether the truth was so difficult to accommodate that she had subjected the whole memory to repression. A related mechanism, the splitting of responsibility off from her father on to those in authority who kept her from home, was also shown by Susan. These are mechanisms of defence. So, too, is the projection of blame from herself to others at the time that she was angry. When she feared that the school counsellor might have designs upon her, she was externalizing a fearful and preoccupying state in her own mind, thereby relieving the inner turmoil.

Anna Freud stressed the capacity of the mind to gain freedom from its most destructive aspects, by endowing skills, talents, and academic and creative capacities with the energy of the drives in such a way that the original instinctual elements are much reduced. This process may begin by the rather superficial processes of rationalizations or intellectualizations (both defence mechanisms) which are relatively ineffective in protecting a child from carrying out unruly impulses. Later, however, sublimation can occur, giving the child opportunities to enjoy and create which are extremely powerful bastions against the disturbances deriving from unresolved conflicts. It is the ability to sublimate that protects children from adversity and which Susan tried so hard to maintain at school for many years. Difficulties in sublimation, in children who fail to keep up academically, make them much more prone to behavioural and emotional difficulties in school and at home.

Anna Freud pointed out that the control of affects, especially the toleration of anxiety and pain, was an important ego function. Some affects are overwhelmingly intolerable, but, in time children have to develop the capacity to cope with separation worries, shaming experience, narcissistic 'wounds', appropriate levels of guilt, and so on. Many children in difficulties suffer because these ego capacities have failed to develop, either because the child has encountered excessive traumas or because of interferences from innate incapacity or from conflicts deriving from previous experiences. Clearly, Susan suffered from overwhelming trauma, and, on the whole, her ego capacities to manage and modulate her feelings were good. Overwhelming sadness and the acting out of a fantasy of reunion with her father in heaven produced her risky suicidal thoughts.

THE CONTRIBUTION OF MELANIE KLEIN

Melanie Klein began her work with children in Berlin and continued in London. Her career began two decades before Freud's death and initially she used a language that expressed the common ground of psychoanalysis. For the purposes of summarizing her work it is possible to divide it into two: first, her exploration of the development of the drives, and second, her re-evaluation of the psychological importance and evolution of children's relation to people (known for historical reasons as 'object relations').

In regard to the drives, Klein extended the notion of an aggressive drive. Freud[14] had suggested the idea of a drive that powered death wishes both against others and the self. He postulated this drive (existing in parallel to the libido) out of observations of the pervasiveness of the cruelty and destructiveness of humankind. (He also adumbrated some more technical reasons for this idea.) He toyed with the idea that the aggressive drive had, as its aim, the death of the self. Klein advocated these notions. She suggested that the mind was structured to deal with a mass of primitive destructive and sexual wishes which were formed into unconscious fantasies that persisted throughout life, being gradually harnessed by the ego. Most of those who work with children in trouble, and especially with those who are very disturbed, will have ample and daily proof of the extent to which children are indeed easily able to reveal the richness and urgency of their fantasy life. The obsession with killing, cruel imprisonment, torture, and injuries is quite overt. The interest in sexuality in all its forms is obvious in the drawings and play of such children. In keeping with the analytic tradition, Klein observed the playing of children with great seriousness and so invented the distinctive component of modern child psychotherapy.

Klein challenged the thinking of her psychoanalytic contemporaries by seeing in the earliest activities of babies evidence of aggressive and sexual fantasies. She also thought that very little children suffered considerably from high levels of anxiety, implying that they could not distinguish such fantasies from reality. All this, I am suggesting, can be seen as Klein's contribution to psychoanalytic drive theory and the content of the id.

However, another element came to preoccupy Klein's clinical theory. She proposed that even very little children had an innate knowledge of their parents' sexual life and also felt envious of and excluded from it. For classical psychoanalysts it was revolutionary to propound the idea that babies related, from the beginning, to the world as though they were aware of people, albeit in a rudimentary way. However, Klein came to suggest an innate origin for the envy that they felt and for its direction towards the mother's ability to feed her babies and the father's possession of procreative capacities.

Klein thus identified children as *relating to objects from the beginning*. She furthermore identified two crises in development that accrued from her drive theory and from the view of early object relatedness. The first crisis, in the first 6 months of life, came about as the child attempted to cope with its innate aggression and envy. Klein suggested that these dangerous feelings, embodied in primitive fantasies, were terrifying to the baby, who tried to cope with them by 'putting them into the outside world' – that is to say by the use of the defence mechanism of projection. These relieved the baby from believing him- or herself to be possessed by such horrible thoughts. At the same time it made the outside world seem an extremely dangerous place, filled as it became clearer with the most destructive and perilous visions. This Klein described, using a phrase originating from W. R. D. Fairbairn[15] as the paranoid-schizoid position. She was of the opinion that such processes were never entirely eliminated from the mind, but might occur in day-dreams, night dreams, symptoms, or breakdowns throughout life. They certainly are fantasies of a type that very disturbed children readily reveal in their relations with family and teachers.

Klein believed that the normal course of events, if a child had a reasonable mothering experience, was for the paranoid-schizoid anxieties to ameliorate as the child became able to distinguish reality and fantasy and as the child had convincing evidence of love and care from surrounding adults. However, the normal course of events ensures that as the child comes to appreciate more the nature of the outside world and his or her own feelings, she or he realizes that the loving adults are or have been the recipients of the earlier intense and destructive fantasies. A characteristic crisis (the 'depressive position') arises with the realization on the part of the child of his or her capacity to damage those who are also most loved and needed (Klein postulated this as occurring in the second half of the first year of life). Such a crisis is never totally resolved and all children can be seen either to suffer from the realization that they can hurt those they love or they can be seen trying to avoid such a realization.

Susan, being in possession of such a dangerous secret about her family, was especially vulnerable to pangs of sadness and guilt that resembled the anxieties of the depressive position. Their importance was that the pain derived not just from the present but was coloured by feelings that derived from earlier times of life when it had been more difficult to get them into more realistic perspective.

THE CONTRIBUTION OF D. W. WINNICOTT

There has continued to be a varied reception within the psychoanalytic world of Melanie Klein's views. On the one hand she has given rise to a strong and evolving school of psychoanalytic practice and theory. However, there is no dispute about the importance of object relations for the understanding and treatment of children. The work of the English psychoanalyst/paediatrician, Donald Winnicott[16] will be mentioned, first as an illustration of another line of the development of psychoanalytic thinking about children, and second, to exemplify the current acceptance of the importance of object relations.

Winnicott, like his great contemporary John Bowlby,[17] was trained within the school of Melanie Klein. Like Bowlby, Winnicott devoted his life to understanding the development of children in relation to their mother. Both provide, in their very different ways, essential ingredients in the understanding of children in difficulties.

Winnicott regarded the mother–child relationship as so important that he thought that it was scarcely possible to consider the baby as a separate entity. He believed that a pregnant woman usually develops a special state of preparedness for taking a child into her life. This leads to a tie between mother and baby whereby the baby's needs are communicated and understood with great precision. This enables the child to survive biologically and protects the baby from a psychological awareness of its own vulnerability and frailty. Gradually, the good-enough mother ensures that she 'fails' the child in a special way. She does this by not responding immediately to the child, beginning instead to show the child that she herself has needs. This enables the baby to come to a realization of the mother and her- or himself as separate people. The realization must come slowly and gently so that the baby is not overwhelmed by feelings of inadequacy and unimportance, and fears of annihilation. This process can go wrong in two ways. The first is that the mother meets the child's needs inadequately and withdraws help too abruptly. This leads the child to be left with a sense of the world as an unfair, unwelcome, and hostile place. Many children in difficulties, usually called deprived, have been let down in this way.

The second way that the process can go wrong is that the mother (and/or father) is too accurate in provision for the child and delays too long in necessary failure to provide what the child needs. She or he failed to bring to the child's awareness that the parent is a separate being. The parent thus deprives the child of a clear knowledge of the nature of the external world and also prevents the child learning skills of self-care and sustenance. To those who work with children, the picture will be familiar. The child is in some ways quite grown up in speech and interests and at the same time it is babyish, demanding, and unconcerned with the needs of others. Such children are especially at risk when the parents grow tired of the spoiling they have induced or when a sib is born.

Winnicott had enormous sensitivity for the way that the relationship ('the space') between child and mother is used by both for their separate but intimately entwined personalities. He showed that this space is used by both and corresponds to a crucial area of mental life that is engaged in nurturing, teaching, and helping children.

CONCLUSIONS

There are many other psychoanalytic contributors who work with children. The purpose of this chapter has been to outline both the range and the development of psychoanalytic ideas. Susan was a suffering, a disturbed adolescent. In her plight she showed many of the features that illustrate the nature of the psychoanalytic approach to disturbed children. She was not delinquent (though she believed that she was being treated as such), nor was she psychotic (although at times she feared that she was going mad). Psychoanalysis has contributed to understanding both of these difficulties but the general principles for understanding them are partially expressed in the account of Susan.

NOTES

1 C. Dare, 'Psychoanalytic theories of development', in M. Rutter and L. Hersov (eds) *Child and Adolescent Psychiatry*, 2nd edn, Oxford: Blackwell Scientific Publications, 1985, p. 204.

2 C. Dare, 'Psychoanalytic marital therapy', in N. S. Jacobson and A. S. Gurman (eds) *Clinical Handbook of Marital Therapy*, New York: Guilford, 1986, Chapter 2, pp. 13–28.

3 See J. J. Sandler, C. Dare, and A. Holder, 'Frames of reference in psychoanalytic psychology: III. A note on the basic assumptions', *British Journal of Medical Psychology* 45 (1972): 143–7.

4 J. Sandler, A. Holder, and C. Dare, 'Frames of reference in psychoanalytic psychology: V. The topographical frame of reference: the organization of the mental apparatus', *British Journal of Medical Psychology* 45 (1973): 29–36.

5 C. Dare, 'Psychoanalytic family therapy', in W. Dryden and E. Street (eds) *Family Therapy in Britain*, Milton Keynes: Open University Press, 1988, p. 24.

6 J. Sandler, A. Holder, and C. Dare, 'Frames of reference in psychoanalytic psychology: IV. The affect–trauma frame of reference', *British Journal of Medical Psychology* 45 (1972): 265–72.

7 J. J. Sandler, C. Dare, and A. Holder, *The Patient and the Analyst*, London: George Allen & Unwin, 1973.

8 Cf. L. Pincus and C. Dare, *Secrets in the Family*, London: Faber and Faber, 1978.

9. See M. M. R. Khan, 'The concept of cumulative trauma', in *The Privacy of the Self*, London: The Hogarth Press, 1974 (orig. 1963), pp. 42–58.

10 V. Smirnoff, *The Scope of Child Analysis*, London: Routledge & Kegan Paul, 1971.

11 A. M. Johnson, 'Sanctions of superego lacunae in adolescents', in D. B. Robinson (ed.) *Experience, Affect and Behavior: Psychoanalytic Explorations of Dr. Adelaide McFayden Johnson*, Chicago: The University of Chicago Press, 1969 (orig. 1949), pp. 113–44.

12 A. Freud, *The Ego and the Mechanisms of Defence*, London: The Hogarth Press, 1939 (orig. 1936).

13 Cf. H. Hartmann, *Ego Psychology and the Problem of Adaptation*, London: The Hogarth Press, 1939; and H. Hartmann, *Essays on Ego Psychology*, London: The Hogarth Press, 1950.

14 S. Freud, 'The Ego and the Id', *Standard Edition* 19 (1923).

15 W. R. D. Fairbairn, *Psychoanalytic Studies of the Personality*, London: Tavistock Publications, 1952.

16 D. W. Winnicott, *The Child and the Family*, London: Tavistock Publications, 1957; D. W. Winnicott, *Collected Papers: Through Paediatrics to Psycho-Analysis*, London: The Hogarth Press, 1958; and D. W. Winnicott, *The Maturational Process and the Facilitating Environment*, London: The Hogarth Press, 1965.

17 J. Bowlby, *Attachment and Loss. Volume I: Attachment*, London: The

Hogarth Press, 1969; J. Bowlby, *Attachment and Loss. Volume II: Separation Anxiety*, London: The Hogarth Press, 1973; and J. Bowlby, *Attachment and Loss. Volume III: Sadness and Depression*, London: The Hogarth Press, 1980.

Chapter Three

BEHAVIOURAL APPROACHES TO THE MANAGEMENT OF CHILDREN WITH EMOTIONAL AND BEHAVIOURAL DIFFICULTIES

JEAN E. SAMBROOKS

At some stage in their lives all children are likely to experience emotional and behavioural difficulties. Behavioural difficulties and emotional difficulties usually go hand in hand as emotional problems are often expressed via behaviour and even those behaviour problems with no overt abnormal emotional drive are often followed by emotional consequences or reactions.

During pre-school and primary school it has been suggested[1] that, on average, boys and girls will experience five or six problems at any one time. The prevalence declines towards the end of the primary school years but at all ages boys tend to have more problems than girls. Secondary-school attendance is often associated with an upsurge of prevalence figures for a year or so and then the decline continues. However, although problems are therefore common they need not necessarily be ignored. The dividing line between a 'problem' behaviour and an acceptable behaviour is one of degree and tolerance; how often is it a problem and to whom, and what difficulties does it cause?

Children with emotional behavioural difficulties present a challenge to the health-care professional not only in terms of the appropriate therapeutic techniques to offer for the particular child and his or her family, but also, and equally importantly, in the initial identification of the nature of a problem. Indeed, accurate assessment of the nature of the problem is a vital precursor to any therapeutic intervention and particularly so for a behavioural approach.

Behavioural approaches are based upon a broad range of work in the fields of social-learning theory, learning theory, and

41

experimental psychology in general. The philosophy of the approach draws on the early conditioning theories exemplified by such workers as Hull and Pavlov and later incorporated into therapeutic approaches to behaviour by Wolpe,[2] Eysenck,[3] Skinner,[4] and many others. Many behavioural approaches, however, go beyond the strict limitations of conditions and principles as characterized by the radical behavioural therapists in the 1950s and adopt a social-learning theory approach.[5] Within this approach not only do the principles of classical and operational conditioning play a part in determining and contributing to an individual's response patterns but the cognitive mediational processes also take on an important role.

Any behavioural approach to the treatment of a child with emotional and behavioural difficulties should take into account the child's developmental history in terms of past learning experiences, the family and significant environment of the child in terms of its role in maintaining the child's difficulties, and the internal mediating processes ongoing in the child and its family members that may also contribute to maintenance of the problem.

A behavioural approach draws upon many fields of knowledge concerned with human behaviour and human development: what characterizes the approach, however, is its commitment to a problem-solving approach[6] and its focus on the actual behaviour of the child and its family. A behavioural approach, therefore, accepts the possibility of an underlying cause for the child's difficulties in its past history and relationship. However, it does not look to the identification of this cause as the means of changing the child's current behaviour but focuses on the factors maintaining the current situation and how these can be altered. It therefore follows that the initial task in a behavioural approach focuses heavily on the assessment of the emotional and behavioural difficulties. However, before moving on to consideration of Phase I – the assessment phase – it is important to consider what is implied by the term 'emotional and behavioural' difficulties.

EMOTIONAL AND BEHAVIOURAL DIFFICULTIES

For the purposes of this chapter it is necessary to consider briefly what the term 'emotional and behavioural difficulties' represents to the present author. A behavioural or emotional difficulty does not usually refer to an emotion or a behaviour that, in itself, constitutes a problem; rather, the effects of the emotion or the behaviour on the child, on the family, and/or on the environment are the real difficulties. An unpleasant emotion is disturbing and therefore difficult for the child him- or herself, or the behaviour is difficult for those around the child in that it may disturb, annoy, or worry them – but frequently the behaviour itself apparently fails to worry the child showing the behaviour – indeed, the behaviour may have a function currently for that child.

The term 'emotional or behavioural difficulty' may therefore refer to a wide range of difficulties including anxiety, depression, aggression, poor concentration, and so on, and can be better characterized by a framework that considers the difficulties in the context of the social, emotional, and behavioural environment of the child. Kauffman's[7] definition of children with behaviour disorders as those 'who chronically and markedly respond to their environment in socially unacceptable and or personally unacceptable unsatisfying ways, but who can be taught more socially acceptable and personally satisfying behaviour' can easily be applied to emotional difficulties and is well expanded in Laslett's book.[8]

PHASE I – THE ASSESSMENT PHASE

Assessing the nature of the child's difficulties is the most time-consuming and meticulous area of assessment and therapy. As such it can be exceedingly frustrating for parents, child, and school, who may be calling for immediate action; and similarly, it is a difficult area for the therapist to research adequately whilst resisting the pressures to offer some panacea to the distressed child and family coping with the difficulties. One of the most effective ways of avoiding these initial difficulties is to ensure adequate explanation to the child and parents in order to encourage co-operation but not influence existing variables in the child's environment.

Assessing whether a problem exists or not also requires a clear idea of the relevant variables used in making such a decision and a large number of factors have to be taken into consideration.

(a) Frequency of occurrence: one child referred to clinic was showing a fairly severe behavioural response of self mutilation when arguments occurred with his father. On occasions spaced weeks apart, he attempted to inflict cuts on his arms, put glass in his eye, and so on. However, the behaviour was so infrequent as to be extremely difficult to modify in that it was unlikely to be repeated in the foreseeable future and indeed was not repeated during the course of a prolonged assessment/exploration phase. The frequency of occurrence is therefore important in that infrequently occurring behaviour is extremely difficult to assess and modify. An indirect approach therefore seemed a more appropriate way of dealing with this particular behaviour. Consideration with the child of alternative ways of coping with stress allowed the child to use different responses under stress in addition to those already present.

(b) The developmental appropriateness of an emotional or behavioural difficulty is a second factor to be considered. Temper tantrums in a 2 year old are a common and frequent part of the available emotional and behavioural repertoire. As such they are amenable to modification if extreme but the child will, in general, grow beyond them naturally. However, frequent temper tantrums in a 12 year old are a developmentally inappropriate occurrence and warrant more concern.

(c) The social relevance of the emotional or behavioural difficulty is also a relevant factor. One 8 year old was regularly apprehended by the police whilst holding the coins obtained by 'robbing a parking meter' (in his words). He was referred for assessment and therapy in view of the persistence of the behaviour. On close examination, however, it transpired that the child belonged to a group of children living in the same street who all indulged in the same behaviour with the same frequency. The referred child's difficulty, however, was that he was rather less able than the other children both cognitionally and physically and if detection was imminent he was left holding the 'spoils'. The solution to his difficulties, however, lay not in terms of altering the child's own behaviour and thereby causing him to be a 'social misfit', but in offering the family alternative accommodation in an area where the social mores were different.

(d) The intensity of the difficulty must also be considered in terms of labelling a child as having an emotional or behavioural difficulty. Slamming the door in anger is qualitatively different to breaking doors and windows when angry and may merit a less intensive approach, depending on the frequency of the action.

(e) The focus of the difficulty within the child's social environment must also be identified. Is it a pervasive difficulty that is shown to all members of the child's social grouping or are specific individuals targets or triggers for the difficulty? Are particular emotions displayed (anger, sadness) or is the entire emotional range apparent on each occasion? Is the behaviour seen only at home, only at school, only with peers, or does it extend to every setting in which the child exists?

(f) The costs and gains of a behaviour must also be identified. One child of 6 was referred for persistently urinating on his bedroom carpet despite having attained bladder control at an appropriate age. The *cost* to the child was a verbal harangue which was a frequent event in his life but the *gain* (of focused attention from his mother) was not easily achieved by other methods. The emotional costs to his mother and their relationship were, however, great as the urinating triggered extreme forms of rejection and anger towards the child for which she subsequently felt very guilty and sad. The long-term cost to the child was therefore potentially very expensive in that, down the chain of responses, urinating stimulated further rejection ultimately but the immediate reinforcement of excessive attention was likely to maintain the urinating behaviour for the foreseeable future.

The aim, therefore, is to identify to whom the behaviour constitutes a problem. Is it the child, the family, the school, society, or all of these? How often is it a problem and to what extent? What is the nature of the problem itself and is it a deficiency or an excess of a particular response that causes the problems? It is also important to remember that, just as a child's problem may be more of a problem to others rather than the child, similarly it is only one part of the child's whole behaviour, and much of the alternative behaviour may be viewed as normal – the child is therefore only a problem *some* of the time, not *all* his waking life.

After consideration of the preceding factors the next step is to identify a baseline in terms of the frequency of the behaviour that is giving rise to difficulties. Baselines are often difficult to achieve successfully and time must be taken to identify the target behaviour clearly. Statements such as 'when he is naughty' or 'when he is aggressive' are of little value as they are imprecise and may have different meanings for different people. When taking a baseline measure for a child presented as, for example, being aggressive, it is important to describe actions clearly – for example, record when 'a' hit, pushed, or kicked 'b'. Note what, if anything, 'a' was holding when he hit 'b'. Every event should be noted and target behaviours identified initially during interview.

At the same time it is often useful to note the time of day when the behaviours occur, and if possible the sequence of events. Parents will therefore be asked to keep a record not only of frequency and timing and duration of the event or behaviour but also to note down those events that lead up to the behaviour – the antecedents. These may range from getting up late several hours before to a request to borrow a toy immediately before the event.

The behaviour itself, its duration and characteristics, then needs to be noted followed by a record of the consequences of the behaviour, both immediate – shouting, praise, smacking – and long term (for example, not allowed out to play for a week, and so on). Such details are notoriously difficult for parents to assemble and their full co-operation is necessary. It also helps if the baseline is reduced to manageable statements (with room for comment) so that, if necessary, ticks or numbers only need be added and note-taking is therefore reduced to a minimum whilst a useful record is obtained.

Accurate baselines are also very important in deciding the next course of action. One family, for example, appeared at clinic complaining that their 4 year-old son frequently hit his younger sibling. However, the baseline record showed that all hitting began after 6 p.m. and was not necessarily uni-directional! At this time the single mother was always washing up the dinner things. Moving the washing-up to a post-bedtime time so significantly reduced the number of hits that the behaviour was no longer noted as a problem.

Having successfully recorded a baseline then consideration need be given as to whether a fairly simple intervention, such as rearranging schedules, within the home or elsewhere (as in the previous example) or reassurance and support, may not be appropriate and effective therapeutic interventions. Parents who are concerned about the abnormality of their child's behaviour may be generating or maintaining it by their anxiety. Children who are worried about aspects of their own behaviour, or the family situation, may similarly need reassurance. Where, however, these rearrangements and reassurances do not seem sufficient for the family's needs, then a categorization of behaviour that indicates the type of intervention available provides a useful framework within which one can organize an intervention.

One useful way to categorize behaviour is in terms of whether it is a lack or an excess of a particular type of behaviour. Does the therapist need to devise an intervention designed to acquire a behaviour that is absent – and/or increase and strengthen the frequency of a weak behaviour such as poor social skills, unsuccessful bowel training, lack of co-operative play, or is it concerned with *decreasing* the frequency of unwanted behaviours such as temper tantrums, high activity levels, and so on.

A learning-theory approach starts from the premiss that the objective of the management is to introduce change into the situation – change not only in the child's repertoire but also in the way people respond to the child's behaviour. It is therefore vital that attention is focused on the need of both the family and the child to change rather than all the emphasis being placed specifically on the child itself.

What, then, can learning theory offer to the management of children with emotional and behavioural difficulties. Such children do not form a homogeneous group; rather, their problems span a broad spectrum, and consequently the type of therapy offered is necessarily diverse. Learning theory has therefore been the basis for a wide variety of treatment techniques and the following section will detail some of them.

PHASE 2 – THERAPEUTIC INTERVENTION

Behavioural techniques can be usefully grouped in terms of whether one is trying to *increase* a deficit behaviour or *decrease* an excessive aspect of behaviour, thereby looking at the overt behaviour and the emotional response that accompanies it. Each family, however, requires careful individual attention as undefined application of behaviour tools is almost automatically doomed to fail; in other words there is no arbitrarily prescribed 'formulae' on offer.

Ways of increasing deficit behaviour

Only relatively rarely is positive reinforcement suggested as the preferred therapeutic choice in order to increase a deficit behaviour. More frequently parents are taught how to decrease unwanted behaviours and the focus is therefore on the negative aspects of a child's behaviour. Where the child and his parent(s) already present as having an emotionally unrewarding or destructive relationship this is unlikely to improve the quality of their mutual perception and interaction; focusing instead on the positive aspects of a child's behaviour both forces the parent to look beyond the negative aspects that have dominated the scene and will also contribute to an improvement in their perception of each other.

Positive reinforcement is one means of increasing deficit behaviour – i.e. using grandma's rule (otherwise known as Premack's principle), 'When *you've* done what *I* want you to do *then* you can do what *you* want to do!' until the child understands the contingent relationship of the two areas of behaviour.

What, however, does the term reinforcement mean? A positive reinforcer is any event which, if given, increases the likelihood of the previous behaviour being repeated. If, therefore, a mother hugged her child each time she uttered the word mummy this would increase the likelihood of this word being repeated – provided the child liked being hugged. Similarly, if the child was hugged each time she smacked her mother then this would also increase the frequency of smacking . . . ! If a child dislikes hugs and hugs are given immediately after the child has said mummy then the frequency of the word 'mummy' in the child's vocabulary would drop. If, therefore, a positive reinforcer immediately follows a piece of behaviour, that behaviour is more likely to be repeated.

Reinforcers can be tangible or intangible (sweets or a hug). They can also come from within the child and again may be tangible (threat, television programme) or unseen (self-praise). Reinforcers must also be under the control of the therapist, with everyone in the childs' environment co-operating as far as possible. If a reinforcer is available in quantity then absence of reinforcement will not be noted. It is therefore important to bring everyone who is involved with the child into the therapeutic plan to some extent. By this means control is effected, a degree of 'demand' can be created, and the previous level of available reinforcement can be reduced if necessary – all of which increases the power of the reinforcement.

For a young child in particular, a reinforcer is something that can be given *immediately* a desired behaviour has occurred and can be given in *small* pieces, for example a small piece of chocolate, not a complete chocolate bar. For the older child, stars and such like may be used as reinforcers, but the immediate reinforcement value of a star is small. The stars therefore need to represent some sort of secondary reinforcement such as a small toy, a privilege, time with a parent, and so on. Many a star chart has however been devised without particular reference to the child's opinion of 'stars' and without choosing secondary reinforcers, and has therefore been doomed to fail.

Experience with one child referred to clinic for lack of compliance with mealtime behavioural norms in the family clearly illustrated the dangers of inadequate research. Punishment and episodes of withdrawal of attention had already been used by the child's parents, who had developed very negative feelings towards the child. It was therefore decided to begin by using positive reinforcement of the acceptable behaviour, as it occurred sufficiently often for this to be done. This might also improve the mother–child relationship if she was involved in rewarding the child.

An elaborate system of reinforcement was established in conjunction with the child and his mother and the decision not to use stars was taken, as they held little value. This then took into account the reinforcement value of the stars quite adequately. Behaviour was therefore recorded with red crosses for acceptable behaviour, and black for unacceptable, with acceptable/unacceptable being defined accurately by the parent, not the child. The tally at the end of each meal was then added up and a reinforcement offered if sufficient 'credits' had been achieved. However, when the frequency of *unacceptable* behaviour increased, the child's mother realized that the child was highly motivated to work for black crosses (his favourite colour) and not for red ticks. Changing the colours over had a dramatic effect thereafter on his behaviour.

Timing and frequency are other crucial variables when administering reinforcement. The important attributes of reinforcers and reinforcement are only briefly mentioned here but are well detailed elsewhere in the literature.[9] Older children may be able to accept tokens exchangeable for a delayed reinforcement administered at the end of a day. Younger children particularly look for immediate reinforcement. If a programme has been established to increase a child's over-short attention span then the reinforcement, be it attention, praise, a drink, or whatever, must be given as soon as the agreed time span has passed even if the child is still concentrating! Saying 'just a minute' with its non-reinforcing feelings of disappointment or resentment will *not* act as a reinforcer and is likely to decrease concentration span even if the appropriate reinforcer is provided thereafter. This is often a difficult principle for parents and teachers to put into practice, used as they are to juggling with competing demands on their time – indeed, delaying tactics may be so habitual that only detailed observation/information gathering and demonstration of the techniques is likely to bring the difficulty to the forefront.

Thus, just as it is important to give sufficient time to the information-gathering phase in terms of behaviour, it is similarly important to ensure that reinforcers *are* reinforcing for the child (and not the parent!) and that they are used appropriately. If this does not take place then the behavioural intervention is equally likely to fail.

The frequency with which a reinforcer is offered when using positive reinforcement is also important. Continuous reinforcement, i.e. offering a reinforcer every time a behaviour occurs, is very useful for increasing the frequency of a particular deficit behaviour. However, once the behaviour is established, continuous reinforcement may not be appropriate in maintaining it. Continuous reinforcement is also useful for developing a skill or teaching an unaccustomed behaviour. In such cases the appropriate ways to 'teach' such a behaviour may be through modelling, i.e. demonstration by a valued adult or peer and also through *shaping*. Shaping is a technique whereby behaviour is broken down into small steps and the steps in the chain are built up until the whole behaviour is mastered. Steps may involve such things as breaking down 'inability to dress oneself in the morning' in a child with poor concentration and low independence-needs to the various stages involved such as 'puts on underpants, puts on socks' and rewarding each stage.

Alternatively, continuous reinforcement may be used to increase the strength of a poorly learned infrequent skill. One disturbed and disturbing child was referred for his inability to 'learn' anything in his nursery class. Observation showed that it was impossible to make much comment about his learning problem as he was never observed to sit to a task for longer than 30 seconds once mealtimes were excluded. The prime task for this child, then, was to increase his concentration span (time on target) and then look at his other difficulties! Positive reinforcement in the form of being allowed a few seconds play with some unusual Dinky cars (chosen by the child) was used, and beginning with a baseline of 30 seconds, increases beyond this of 10 seconds at a time of on-target behaviour (naming objects in interesting pictures) were then reinforced, with the eventual result that the child's final on-target behaviour was around 10 minutes – adequate for a child of 3 and sufficient to allow work to commence on his developmental delay.

One last point about reinforcers concerns 'saturation'. Frequent use of positive reinforcement may lead to saturation with the reinforcer, even when it is highly desired and divisible into small pieces.

Menus of reinforcers, however, provide a useful alternative and allow the child to suggest a range of reinforcers which he or she can then choose from when the desired behaviour has occurred. One child, again referred for poor concentration, considered being able to sit on her mother's knee and cuddle for 5 minutes to be the best reinforcer. However, because of her mother's own difficulties this was a difficult reinforcer for the mother to offer. Consequently, a menu was set up whereby cuddling was one available reinforcer, but when that had been 'used' once, alternatives on the menu were worked through until 'cuddling' re-emerged at the top of the list. The alternative choices ranged from playing together with a toy for a period, including two tangible reinforcers of special drinks and fruit, and involved some reinforcers being given by the father rather than the mother, which also increases the generalizability and power of the reinforcement.

Negative reinforcement is also a way of increasing a desired behaviour, and also decreasing an undesired one. Many parents use it frequently without applying behavioural labels at the meal table (a frequent source of difficulties in a family!). At such times some children become extremely attention seeking, play act, are noisy, and so on; banishing them to another room or removing oneself and one's dinner to another room are effective ways of applying negative reinforcement in that the child looses attention whenever his or her behaviour becomes unacceptable. Acceptable behaviour may however earn the child positive reinforcement of increased attention and strengthen the likelihood of the behaviour being repeated.

Frequently, behavioural change is achieved by a whole process of rearranging contingencies for the family using both positive and negative reinforcement. This allows for concentration on various aspects of behaviour within the family and the possibility of conceptual changes occurring across the participants.

Use of both procedures enables one to use escape and/or avoidance training together with positive reinforcement or deprivation of reinforcement, and allows for considerable flexibility in the programme.

Weakening undesired behaviour

If a child persistently behaves in an undesirable way then he or she is being rewarded for this in some way – even if the nature of the reward is obscure. What we might regard as punishing or unpleasant may not be seen in this way by the child. Again this underlines the importance of initial information-gathering with the child and family to understand what does or does not constitute reinforcement.

If the child continues to show frequent episodes of an undesirable behaviour – such as swearing, tantrums, or perhaps persistent interruptions – then it may be necessary to consider trying to alter his or her behaviour in order to reduce the frequency of the incidents. At the same time, however, it is important that alternative behaviours are also reinforced to help the child substitute an appropriate behaviour.

One method of effecting change is by ignoring it (ostentatiously if necessary!), i.e. clearly *not* responding and therefore *NOT* reinforcing the undesirable behaviour. When confronted with a child who persistently demands your attention, *especially* if you are occupied preparing dinner or answering the telephone, then ignoring the child entirely at these times will be non-reinforcing and the behaviour will eventually decrease. Initially, however, it is likely to increase in frequency as the child is used to having his or her pestering attended to successfully some of the time. Failing to get attention will therefore cause him to try harder initially but after a period the behaviour will begin to reduce. Ignoring, however, is hard and many parents have adopted techniques to help them ignore – for example, one mother would pull on a woolly hat and become 'deaf'; another would whistle, a third would offer a long, boring monologue of the complexity of the job being undertaken!

Ignoring or extinction of a learned response often entails the involvement of others. There is little point in one parent ignoring a child's attention-seeking behaviour, be it swearing, slamming doors, and so on, if granny can be relied upon to comment upon it! Or if one nurse in a nursery has agreed to try ignoring a child when it commences a piercing high pitched wail, then all the nurses, ancillary staff, and so on must also be involved, or else attention will be forthcoming from someone.

As has already been mentioned, ignoring can also lead to an initial reduction and then temporary resurgence of the behaviour, outcomes which need to be predicted and therefore anticipated by the parent as otherwise, discouragement may cause the intervention to fail. Ignoring a child is only possible, however, with a behaviour that it is possible to ignore. Some behaviours, be they intense fear reactions, destructive aggressive responses, or very persistent, hard-to-ignore ones, cannot be ignored, and alternatives for managing the behaviour should be considered. If ignoring should fail to work, it should also be questioned whether attention was the prime reinforcer for the behaviour or whether it was an alternative unidentified reinforcer.

'Time-out' is a more pervasive way of removing reinforcement and is more appropriate for those behaviours one cannot easily ignore. It is not appropriate, however, if a child finds it an unbearable situation and should not be used for children who can entertain themselves happily by singing and so on in this time, or children whose problems are partly related to their inability to mix with others.

Time-out is a technique involving the removal of the child to a boring uninteresting place such as the bottom stair, or the hall, or even a chair in the room. The child is told the 'rules' – for example, 'If you scream/swear you go to time-out.' If the behaviour persists the child is removed to the time-out area and remains there for a very short time – no more than 2–3 minutes for young children and no more than 5–10 minutes for older children. The time-out situation is meant to be intensely boring and devoid of stimulation but not a frightening place in any way. It is meant to be a place to 'cool off', to regain control over oneself, and some children do find it just that and may even ask for time-out if upset. Others, however, see it as a punishment and cannot see the positive side of it.

For a younger child, sent to time-out for screaming perhaps, then time-out can cease almost the moment the child is quiet. If the child begins again as soon as she is out of time-out, however, then she immediately returns to time-out for another period. As with ignoring it is vitally important to involve others so that they do not invalidate time-out and it is important to model the removal to *and* from time-out.

One referral of a small child, threatened with expulsion (at the age of 4) from his nursery class, clearly illustrates the necessity of modelling. Johnny was referred for throwing chairs at other children, swearing, spitting, fighting, and breaking toys. On frequent occasions refusal to comply with a reasonable request was followed by the child barricading himself behind a line of chairs, swearing, and throwing one at anyone who came near. Time-out was therefore suggested as the behaviour was difficult for the other children and the time-out area chosen was just outside the nursery door. The technique was modelled but seemed to have little effect until it was observed that teachers from other rooms would pass the door and comment to the child, thereby providing positive reinforcement of the non-acceptable behaviour. Similarly, although modelling of time-out had been demonstrated, the return had not, and consequently the child would remain in time-out for the allotted time even if his behaviour (for example, screaming) had ceased long before. Changes were therefore effected, all staff involved, and the time-out area changed to the main office which had few distractions but a person to keep an eye on this young child.

No one in the nursery now discussed time-out directly when the child was in time-out but the procedure was still ineffective, and indeed the number of time-outs needed was increasing. A colleague observed that every visitor to the office would be given an account of why the child was there – no one actually spoke *to* him! – and a considerable amount of vicarious attention was forthcoming which had not been identified when querying the procedures. This was also dealt with, time-out then worked extremely effectively, and all tantrums ceased within a couple of weeks. At the same time positive reinforcement of more stimulating interactive play in small groups was offered which reduced the boredom factor and offered the opportunity to learn to share.

Punishment, in its many variations, is also a way to reduce undesirable behaviour and is frequently used by parents to control behaviour problems. Punishment does not only mean hitting and smacking but also scolding, shouting, and so on. Punishment in this form, with an aversive response immediately following the undesirable behaviour, is effective in the short term in that it tends to suppress the behaviour. However, it does not weaken the strength of the response and the behaviour is therefore likely to be repeated as the pleasurable consequences have usually reinforced the behaviour prior to the aversive event. Children also habituate to the aversive event and therefore the tendency to smack a little harder may creep in, particularly in parents who feel powerless.

Making the difficult behaviour *cost* in different ways is also an often used alternative whereby the child loses desirable reinforcers and privileges if she shows an identified undesirable behaviour. The technique can also be used as a negative reinforcer to increase deficit behaviour such as co-operative behaviour (for example, doing the chores). The effectiveness of this behaviour is dependent on a balance of response cost vs. the positive reinforcement value attracted to the behaviour itself: for example, 'stay out late, early in for a week' may not be effective in changing behaviour if the one evening out beyond the agreed time is very highly valued.

Excess behaviours are not necessarily antisocial, nonconforming behaviours. They may also be anxiety or fear responses which may affect behaviour in a variety of ways, for example not going to school because of the fear of school. Fear in this situation then engenders an avoidance response whereby the child is unable to attend school, never experiences the school situation, and therefore never exposes the fear to the situation which might resolve it or extinguish it. Various behavioural options exist to cope with excessive anxiety: flooding is one extreme which involves keeping children in contact with the *most* feared object until the fear extinguishes – for example, taking them to school, placing them in the most feared situation in school (for example, reading out loud to an insensitive teacher), and getting them to continue this until the fear subsides and they realize everything is still normal, thereby associating coping with the situation and not fear. Flooding, however, whilst effective, is difficult to carry out with children from the therapists' viewpoints as it is unclear whether they can understand the reasoning behind the therapy, it can be a distressing experience, and may appear to be a punishment for the avoidance response.

Systematic desensitization is an alternative way of dealing with an excessive fear response. In this technique the child is gradually exposed to the feared situation whilst simultaneously pairing the exposure with a response incompatible with fear – sometimes a relaxation response, sometimes play or reward, or sometimes the presence of trusted supportive person or therapist.

One child referred at the age of 8 had a severe fear of fire which had developed from the age of 5 years. This fear now extended to being unable to be in the same room as candles on a birthday cake; high flames on the gas ring; running out of school sobbing with fear when a painter's blowtorch was used on a distant wall; being unable to visit the dentist (with his sterilizing flame), a camp (butane camp cooker), bonfire night, and so on. The child dreamt of fires, was consistently worried that his parents, who smoked, would burn to death, and stayed at home, not playing with friends to prevent an imaginary fire occurring.

Relaxation was taught briefly and modelled at home by the child's mother. A hierachy was drawn up (and modified as time went on). Imaginary and *in vivo* desensitization was used as the child found visualizing quite hard. Successive exposures were rewarded by playing a favourite game whilst practising breathing exercises (a relaxing and rewarding situation), and over a few weeks the child progressed through lighting matches, blowing out candles, turning on gas rings, to standing near open fires and bonfires, and eventually collecting 'penny for the guy' in order to participate in bonfire night! This degree of independence was a little disquieting for the parents but discussion helped the family adjust to this independent, happy child and a balance was found.

Many variants exist when considering ways of reducing an excessive response of some sort. Modelling in various forms can be extremely effective with children; cognitive and/or behaviour rehearsal of responses; rewarding or teaching alternative behaviours that effectively organize or control the child's environment rather than the excessive anger and fear currently being shown. However, insufficient space exists in this chapter to offer sufficient details for practising such techniques but several good textbooks are already in existence on the subject.[10, 11]

Behavioural techniques are powerful tools if used appropriately and can be very useful ways of effecting change in children with emotional and behavioural problems. All therapies are about change in one form or another and behavioural techniques are one possibility for the therapist. They cannot effect change, however, without the knowledge and consent of the people involved and require close co-operation between child and family if effective change is to be achieved. Rigorous attention to existing contingencies and reinforcers, adequate baseline measures, and detailed information are however vital if the therapy is to be effective.

NOTES

1 J. W. MacFarlane, L. Allen, and M. P. Honzik, *A Developmental Study of the Behaviour Problems of Normal Children Between Twenty Two Months and Fourteen Years*, Berkeley: University of California Publications in Child Development Vol. 11, University of California Press, 1954.
2 J. Wolpe, *Psychotherapy by Reciprocal Inhibition*, Stanford: Stanford University Press, 1958.
3 H. J. Eysenck, 'Learning theory and behaviour therapy', *J. of Ment. Sc.* 105 (1959): 61–75.
4 B. F. Skinner, *Science and Human Behaviour*, New York: MacMillan, 1953.
5 A. Bandura, *Principles of Behaviour Modification*, New York: Holt, 1969.
6 W. Yule, 'Behavioural approaches', in M. Rutter (ed.) *Scientific Foundations of Developmental Psychiatry*, London: Heinemann, 1985.
7 J. M. Kauffman, *Characteristics of Children's Behaviour Disorders*, Ohio: Charles E. Merrill, 1977.
8 R. Laslett, 'Changing perceptions of maladjusted children 1945–1981', Sussex: Association of Workers for Maladjusted Children, 1983.
9 O. M. Gelfand and D. P. Hartman, *Child Behaviour – Analysis and Therapy*, New York: Pergamon Press, 1975.
10 Ibid.
11 M. Herbert, *Behavioural Treatment of Problem Children – A Practice Manual*, London: Academic Press, 1981.

Chapter Four

THE PSYCHIATRIC EXAMINATION OF CHILDREN WITH EMOTIONAL AND BEHAVIOURAL DIFFICULTIES

PHILIP BARKER

The psychiatric examination of a child requires that both the child be interviewed and the child's family and wider social environment be assessed. Children are dependent upon those caring for them and there are often found to be marked differences in the behaviour and adjustment of children in different situations, for example at home, in school, or in sports groups or clubs. Only a small minority of children identified as disturbed at home are similarly identified in school and vice versa.

The sequence in which the interviews are carried out is optional. I often start by seeing the whole family, following which I interview the child. I then usually see the parent(s) on their own. With younger children this generally works well, but adolescents are sometimes best seen on their own before anyone else is interviewed. This applies especially when the young person is the subject of intense criticism or negative attitudes on the part of other family members. Otherwise they may feel, often rightly, that they have been reported on unfavourably by others before they have been able to state their point of view. While unfavourable reports may be made, or hostile feelings expressed, during a family interview, the young person does at least know what has been said and can express differing views. This is usually better than feeling you are being spoken about behind your back.

INTERVIEWING THE FAMILY

A diagnostic family interview should proceed through stages. These are:

— Making the initial contact with the family.
— Joining the family and establishing rapport.
— Defining the problems and reaching agreement on the desired outcome.
— Reviewing the family's history and its current developmental stage; the construction of a genogram is invaluable here.
— Assessing the current functioning of the family.

These stages are not mutually exclusive and several may be in process at the same time. Thus, for example, the establishment and enhancement of rapport should continue as long as there is contact with the family.

The initial contact

If the whole family is to be interviewed as part of the initial assessment, it should be made clear, when the appointment is made, that all family members in the household should attend. If family members question the necessity of this, points that may be made include:

— It is easier to gain a proper understanding of a child's problems if you are familiar with that child's family setting.
— The behaviour of any one family member inevitably affects the other members.
— The other family members can often be part of the solution to the problem. (It is seldom helpful to suggest that they are a part of the problem itself.)

It is usually easy to persuade parents that *they* are important to their children, but they may be reluctant to bring siblings whom they consider to be well-adjusted and problem-free; in that case you may point out that the well-functioning children may have much to offer the 'problem' child, in that they have acquired the skills to function well in the family – skills the identified patient needs.

Joining the family and establishing rapport

Rapport may be defined as a state of understanding, harmony, and accord. Trust usually accompanies it. The establishment of rapport should start with the initial contact, and it should be a prime objective in the initial interviews, both with the child and with the family group.

Establishing rapport has been given other names, such as 'joining' the family[1] or 'building working alliances'.[2] As it develops, the participants become increasingly involved with each other. When rapport is well developed the interviewer can say almost anything, even quite outrageous things, without the client becoming upset; remarks which could be construed as insulting will be taken as meant jokingly, or at least not seriously.

Non-verbal means of promoting rapport include the matching or 'pacing' of the behaviour of those being interviewed. This is achieved by adopting the same body postures, movements, respiratory rhythm, speed of talking, and voice tone and volume. Behaviour can also be 'mirrored' or 'cross-matched'. Mirroring is the moving of, say, your left arm or leg in response to similar movements of the client's right arm or leg. 'Cross-matching' occurs, for example, when the therapist's hand or finger is moved in rhythm with movements of the person's foot. Movements which may be matched include the crossing and uncrossing of the subject's legs, the tilting of the head to one side or the other, and leaning forward or settling back.

If pacing is done sensitively and unobtrusively, those being paced do not become consciously aware of it. Indeed, it is behaviour which occurs spontaneously whenever people are in a state of rapport, whatever the situation. It is not unique or specific to clinical interviews.

It is only necessary to match certain of the behaviours of those being interviewed, and of course it is not possible to pace simultaneously the behaviours of all members of a family, though you may observe common factors about their behaviour which you can use. With families it is usually sufficient to match the behaviours of the different family members in turn, perhaps as you speak to each one.

Verbal means of promoting rapport include matching your predicates with those used by your clients.[3,4] A predicate is a word that says something descriptive about the subject of a sentence: predicates include verbs, adjectives, and adverbs.

Some people use mainly visual, rather than auditory or feeling, predicates – as in the sentences 'I see what you mean', or 'Things are looking brighter.' Examples of the use of auditory predicates are: 'I hear what you're saying', 'That sounds terrible', or 'It was like music to my ears.' Sentences such as 'I have a lot of heavy problems', 'That feels like a good idea', or 'That's a big weight off my shoulders' illustrate the use of 'kinesthetic' or feeling-type predicates. Although we all use predicates of all three types – as well as some olfactory ('This business smells fishy to me') and gustatory ('It leaves a bad taste in my mouth') ones, and many that are non-specific, most of us have a preferred way of processing information, using one of the three main sensory channels. Noting this, and using the information to 'join' others in processing information as they do, is a powerful rapport-building technique.

In addition to matching predicates, you should listen carefully to the vocabularies of those you are interviewing, especially children, noting the words and expressions they use. Few things impede the establishment of rapport as much as repeatedly using words and expressions with which those to whom you are speaking are unfamiliar. Methods of establishing and enhancing rapport are discussed further in Chapter 3 of my *Basic Child Psychiatry*.[5]

Defining the desired outcome

Almost invariably, children are brought for psychiatric examination because someone is seeking some change. This may be in the child's behaviour, emotions, school performance, relationships with others, mental or physical development, or whatever. Defining, and if necessary clarifying, the changes sought is important for several reasons:

— It formally acknowledges the family's concerns.
— It defines your involvement as therapeutic and oriented towards promoting change.
— It helps avoid misunderstandings about the purpose of the child's or the family's attendance.
— It provides an opportunity for the family members to clarify their thoughts, and if necessary to consider the situation they

do want, rather than complaining about how they do not like the present one.

— It can inspire hope by having the family look forward to a better future, rather than dwelling upon the past.

— If all, or even several, family members are present it offers an opportunity for them to discover whether they all have the same objectives.

— There is no way to define success if no desired outcome has been established.

Therapeutic goals should be defined in positive, rather than negative terms. It is not sufficient for parents to say they want their child's tantrums to cease; they should be asked how they would like the child to react in situations in which tantrums have been occurring. Other points to consider are:

— What consequences will follow once the goals have been achieved?

— Are there any drawbacks which may be associated with these consequences?

— Under what circumstances are the changes desired? Most behaviours have value in some situations.

— What has prevented the changes occurring in response to whatever has been tried so far?

— How quickly should the changes occur? Change that is too rapid can itself be stressful and adjusting to new situations takes time. There is also embedded in this question the idea that change *will* occur.

The establishment of treatment goals is discussed in more detail in Chapter 6 of my *Basic Family Therapy*.[6]

Reviewing the family's history, determining its developmental stage, and constructing a genogram

These tasks can conveniently be tackled in a session with the whole family. Ask the parents where they were born and brought up, what kinds of families they were raised in, how they got along at school, and what they did when they left school. Then ask them how they met and courted, and invite them to outline the course of their married life so far.

Enquire next about the births of the children and their development to date. This will tell you what stage in its life cycle the family has reached; there may also have emerged evidence of any difficulty the family is having in passing from one stage to the next.

A *genogram*, or family map, should now be constructed, with the family's active participation. This provides a concise, graphic summary of a family's current composition. It should also show the extended family network, the geographical locations and ages of the various family members, the dates of the parents' marriage, and those of any previous marriages, divorces, or separations; and it indicates how the family members are related. It can also show who is the identified patient, although I prefer to omit this information when I am working on a genogram with family members. Figure 4.1 (reproduced from my *Basic Family Therapy*) provides an example of a genogram.

In this example (a complex family system chosen to illustrate the range of information a genogram can convey), the parents of the identified patient, Brad (distinguished by a double boundary), cohabited in a 'common law' relationship from 1965 to 1969, after which they got married. They separated in 1973 and were legally divorced in 1980. Carmen, Brad's mother, lived with Eric from 1973 to 1976 and they had two daughters, Jane and Audrey. Eric subsequently married Fay and they now have a daughter, Holly. Carmen commenced living with Ken in 1978 and they were married in 1982. Her two children by Eric, and one by Ken, make up their present family unit. Brad and his father, Dave, live with Katrina and her 10-year-old daughter by her former husband, Len. Katrina also had a previous pregnancy which ended in a miscarriage in 1974. Carmen is an only child and both her parents are dead; Dave is the fourth in a family of one girl and four boys.

The current functioning of the family

The way the family members interact with each other and the characteristics of the family system as a whole should be studied. In every family each member has an assigned role. Roles are not usually formally assigned or consciously planned. They develop over the life-span of the family, beginning with the union of the two parents to form a marital couple. The behaviour and emotional states of the family members are however closely related to the roles

Figure 4.1 The Green family genogram, 1985

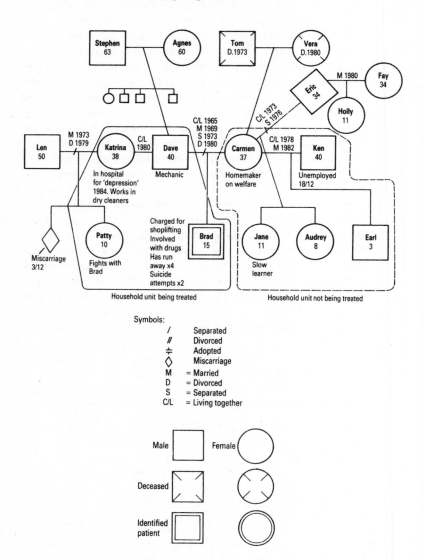

Source: Philip Barker, *Basic Child Psychiatry*, 5th edn, Oxford: Blackwell Scientific, 1988.

each of them has come to play in the family system. The assessment of families is discussed more fully in my *Basic Family Therapy*.

THE CHILD'S HISTORY

At some point a history of the child's development and of the current problems must be obtained. If possible both parents should be involved in providing this. Some of this information may be obtained during the interview with the whole family, some in talking with the parents, and some during the individual interview with the young person.

You should ask about the development of the child's symptoms, their duration and frequency, whether they are getting better or worse or have remained much the same for a while, and how the parents have attempted to deal with them – and with what success.

Areas which have not so far been covered should next be explored. These may include the child's adjustment, behaviour, and progress at school, in the family, or in the wider social environment. The child's past and present physical health should also be reviewed. You should ask about the duration, frequency, and degree of both problem behaviours and strengths. Observe also how parents describe symptoms: do they make light of their child's problem behaviour, or do they describe it in over-dramatic or rejecting terms?

The developmental history

This should cover the following:

— The course of the pregnancy, any complications, whether the mother used alcohol or drugs, and if so, how heavily.
— The child's birth and neonatal condition.
— The subsequent progress of the child's development (motor, speech, feeding, toilet training, social behaviour and adjustment, progress in school, and so on.)
— Any previous illnesses, injuries, or emotional problems.

It is useful to have a description of the child's behaviour as a baby, as a toddler, over the period of starting school, and up to the present time.

EXAMINING THE CHILD

There can be no set routine for the psychiatric examination of children. Much depends on the child's age, language skills, willingness to talk, and personality. Communication with children below the age of 5 is usually mainly through the medium of play, though many pre-school children reveal a lot about themselves in conversation. Older children, and especially adolescents, can often be approached much as adult patients are. In between, both play and conversation are used.

It is seldom the presenting child who is complaining of symptoms. Usually an adult, often a parent or teacher, is either complaining on the child's behalf or is objecting to some aspect of the child's behaviour. Thus, it is best not to start the interview by discussing the presenting complaints; to do so may lead the child to identify you with other disapproving adults, impeding the development of a trusting relationship.

Rapport-building techniques were discussed above. Children should feel that they and their points of view and opinions are respected and valued. The atmosphere in the consulting room should be relaxed and friendly, but not condescending. Toys, play materials, and painting and drawing materials, appropriate to the child's age, should be available. I do not like to have a desk between the child and myself; to do so tends to distance child and interviewer emotionally as well as physically.

Younger children are best seen in a playroom. It should be made clear that the toys and play materials are there for their use. It is often best to invite them to play for a while, rather than immediately initiating a conversation. A conversation may then be started as the child plays.

I prefer to start talking with children about topics well away from the symptom areas, such as how they travelled to the clinic or office, their interests and hobbies, games they like to play, their toys, any recent birthday, school (unless this is an area of difficulty), friends, siblings, and their ambitions for the future. If Christmas, Easter, a holiday, or other such events have occurred recently, these can be discussed.

The symptoms or presenting problems may come up as the interview proceeds; if not, they can be dealt with later. There is little point in asking, 'Did you steal such-and-such?' If the child answers 'yes', the interviewer is usually none the wiser; if 'no', the child has been forced into the position of withholding information. This may damage the developing relationship between interviewer and child. Still less should one say, 'Why did you steal?' Such questions are futile. By asking them you place yourself in the same category as other authority figures who may have been questioning, lecturing, and perhaps punishing the child for his or her behaviour. While you will of course wish to understand why the child has been displaying the problem behaviour, it is naïve to suppose that this can be achieved by asking such questions.

The early part of the first interview, sometimes the whole of it, is thus spent gaining the child's confidence. Once this has been achieved, at least in fair measure, it is justifiable to ask, in a general way, what has brought the child to the clinic, office, or hospital. An accurate reply may be given, but if not the subject should not be pressed.

Once rapport has been established, the various areas of the child's life may be explored. This should be done gently, using words and in a manner appropriate to the child's age and personality. The interview should not be an interrogation. It is more a matter of saying, 'Lots of people have dreams when they are asleep at night . . . I wonder if you do?' The child who admits to having dreams may be invited to recount one, and then perhaps asked whether the dreams are mostly pleasant or unpleasant ones. To the child who denies having or remembering dreams, you may say, 'Often when people who don't have dreams come to see us, they like to make up a dream . . . to pretend they've had one . . . perhaps you'd like to do that?' This is one way of exploring children's fantasy lives. Another is to ask them to imagine they can have three magic wishes and that whatever they wish will come true; what would their three wishes be? Children often take their wishes very seriously. You may then say something like, 'Now I'd like you to pretend you were all alone on a desert island (or in a boat) and you could choose one person to be with you . . . anyone you like but just one person . . . I wonder who you would have?' You may next ask the child to choose a second person, then a third.

You should enquire in a similar way for fears, worries, and somatic and other symptoms. Encourage conversation about family, friends (whom the child can be asked to name and describe), and school, responding appropriately to what the child is saying. Try to share the child's sorrow at the loss of a pet, or pleasure at being a member of a winning sports team. Above all, convey interest in the child's point of view. This does not necessarily imply approval of everything the child does or thinks.

I invite children who have not reached adolescence to draw, paint, and/or play with some of the toys. This enables me to assess their concentration, attention-span, distractibility, and motor dexterity. Much can be learned from the content of their play and their artistic productions. I usually ask any child I see to draw her or his family. The appearances of the different family members, their relative sizes and positions, and even who is included and who is left out, can reveal much. Another useful step is to invite the child to draw a 'person' and then discuss that person. If the child draws a boy, I might ask, 'What makes him happy?', 'What makes him sad?', 'What makes him angry?', 'What makes him laugh?', 'How many friends does he have?', 'Does he make friends easily?', 'Do people like him?' . . . , and so on. The answers may reveal much about the child's view of the world.

We can learn much about children from what they draw, paint, or model. Some pictures bristle with aggression: guns are firing, people are being hurled from buildings or otherwise killed, and violence of various sorts is occurring. Others portray sadness: people are crying, or are shown as feeling ill or even being about to die. Yet other pictures show happy scenes, or illustrate the fulfilment of the artist's ambitions.

The child's artistic productions should be kept with the other clinical records. What children say as they draw, paint, or make models should also be recorded; this helps explain what their productions represent. What they draw, paint, or model must also be interpreted in the light of the whole clinical picture, taking into account all the other available information. *Interpreting Children's Drawings*[7] is a valuable source of further information and refers also to earlier work on the subject.

Adolescents do not always wish to paint, play, or draw, but it is sometimes surprising how readily they accept the invitation to do so. Their productions can be as revealing as those of younger children.

The following are the main points on which observations should be made during the examination of the child.

(1) *General appearance*: Abnormalities of facial appearance, head,

body build, or limbs. Bruises, cuts, or grazes. Mode of dress and appropriateness for the climate and time of year. Attitude to the examiner and the consultation.

(2) *Motor function*: Activity level and nature of motor activities. Are movements performed normally, or clumsily, quickly, or slowly? Abnormal movements such as tics. Right- or left-handed? Can the child distinguish right from left? Abnormalities of gait. Ability to write, draw, and paint.

(3) *Speech*: Articulation, vocabulary, and use of language. Does the child speak freely, little, or not at all? Any stuttering? Receptive and expressive language abilities.

(4) *Content of talk and thought*: The subjects the child chooses to talk about. How easy it is to steer the conversation towards particular topics. Any subjects that are avoided. Whether the child's stream of thought is logical and whether there is any abnormal use of words or expressions. Evidence suggesting that the child is deluded or hallucinated.

(5) *Intellectual function*: A rough estimate may be made, based on general knowledge, conversation, level of play, and knowledge of time, day, date, year, place, and people's identity, taking into account what is normal for the child's age.

(6) *Mood and emotional state*: Happy, elated, unhappy, frankly depressed, anxious, hostile, resentful, suspicious, upset by separation from parents, and so on? Level of rapport which has been established. Has the child ever wanted to run away, or to hide, wished to be dead or contemplated suicide? Does the child cry, and if so, in what circumstances? Specific fears and if present how they are dealt with. Appropriateness of emotional state to subject being discussed.

(7) *Attitudes to family*: Indications during conversation about family members or during play.

(8) *The child's school situation*: Attitudes towards school generally, academic work, play, staff, other pupils. Child's estimate of own abilities and progress in school.

(9) *Fantasy life*: The child's three magic wishes. The three most desired companions on a desert island. Dreams reported or made up. The worst thing – and the best thing – that could happen to the child. The child's ambitions in life. Material expressed in play, drawing, painting, or modelling.

(10) *Sleep*: Difficulty in sleeping. Fear of going to bed or to sleep,

nightmares, night terrors (not usually reported by children unless they have been told they have them by others), pleasant dreams.

(11) *Behaviour problems*: Anything revealed by the child about behaviour problems, delinquent activities, illicit drug use, running away, sexual problems, or appearance in court.

(12) *Placement away from home*: When, where, and for how long. The child's reaction to and understanding of this.

(13) *Attitude to referral*: The child's view of the referral, and the reasons for it.

(14) *Indications of social adjustment*: Number of reported friends, hobbies, interests, games played, youth organizations belonged to, how leisure time is spent. Whether the child feels a follower or a leader, or bullied, teased or picked on, and, if so, by whom?

(15) *Other problems*: Other problems that come to light during the interview, for example worries, pains, headaches, other somatic problems, or relationship difficulties.

(16) *Play*: A general description of the child's play, whether this is symbolic and to what extent. Content of play. Concentration, distractibility, constructiveness.

(17) *The child's self-image*: This is inferred from the sum total of what the child does and says, the ambitions and fantasy ideas expressed, and the child's estimate of what others think of him or her. Disturbed children may overrate their self-esteem, as compared to ratings by parents, therapists, or teachers.[8]

You may not be able to obtain all the above information in one interview, and assessment is an ongoing process, continuing as long as contact with child or family continues. Clearly some of the above categories do not apply to non-speaking children. The fact that a child who can talk declines to do so is of course itself an important clinical observation.

Further information on interviewing and examining children is available in books by Goodman and Sours[9] and Simmons.[10] *Anxiety in Children*[11] contains a chapter on the recognition of anxiety in children by means of psychiatric interview.[12] Research on the validity and reliability of various approaches to interviewing children and parents is reported in a number of publications.[13–20]

The physical examination

A physical examination should be carried out at some point, since there are many physical conditions which may cause or lead to emotional and behavioural disorders. These are discussed in my *Basic Child Psychiatry* (Chapters, 2, 7 and 8) (see note 5). Some psychiatrists prefer to arrange for the physical examination to be done by another physician, believing that the procedure may impede the development of a psychotherapeutic relationship.

OTHER SOURCES OF INFORMATION

It is often important to obtain information from other sources. These may include:

— The child's school.
— Schools the child has attended in the past.
— Mental health professionals who have assessed or treated the child or family in the past.
— Health professionals who are currently involved with child or family.
— Social agencies which have been involved with the child or the family, for example child protection and child welfare agencies and probation services.
— Hospitals and other institutions in which the child has been treated or has received care.
— Foster parents and others who have cared for the child.

The informed consent of the parents must, of course, always be obtained before contact is made with other agencies or professionals.

Aponte, a family therapist, recommended that when the presenting problems concern the child's school situation, the first face-to-face contact should be a family–school interview. This idea has merit, especially when the initiative for referral comes from the school.[21]

OTHER ASSESSMENT MEASURES

Various additional assessment devices may be helpful in adding to the information obtained by interviews as described above. These include the following.

71

Psychological tests

— *Intelligence tests.* These provide a measure of a child's level of cognitive functioning, and of areas of strength and weakness. They are useful when the child's cognitive functioning is in question, as for example when there are academic difficulties at school.

— *Tests of academic attainment.* These measure the child's level of functioning in areas such as reading, spelling, and mathematics.

— *Personality tests.* These include projective tests in which the child is presented with vague or ambiguous material. This may consist of material derived from ink blots (as in the Rorschach Test) or of pictures of varying degrees of ambiguity. The aim is to elicit responses which reflect the subject's personality or mental state. These tests can be helpful in supplementing the information obtained at interview, especially with children who are guarded or do not talk freely to the examiner.

— *Tests of specific psychological functions.* Many other tests are available to assess language development, self-esteem and self-perception, motor development, the presence of emotional disturbance, perceptual skills, temperament, the presence of organic brain damage, and other aspects of children's functioning.

The administration and interpretation of psychological tests is the province of the clinical or educational psychologist, who should be consulted when the information obtained at psychiatric interview is insufficient or its meaning is unclear.

The role of psychological tests and the indications for their use in the assessment of disturbed children are discussed further in Chapter 3 of my *Basic Child Psychiatry* (see note 5).

Other medical tests

These include electroencephalographs (EEGs), X-rays and other methods of diagnostic imaging, and various laboratory tests. None of these is usually necessary if there are no symptoms suggesting organic disease and physical examination reveals no relevant abnormality. When these conditions are not met, however, referral should be made to a paediatrician or neurologist, who may arrange further special tests or investigations. It is important to remember that almost any psychiatric symptom can have an organic cause.

THE FORMULATION

The final step, when the above processes have been completed, is to develop a case formulation. This is a concise summary of the information you have obtained, together with your understanding of how the various factors that have come to light combine to produce the presenting clinical picture.

The formulation should start with a brief statement of the presenting problem(s). As the next step it is often helpful to enter the data on to a grid such as that shown in Figure 4.2.

Predisposing, precipitating, perpetuating, and protective factors should be considered under each of the five headings, covering constitutional, temperamental, physical, psychological, and environmental factors.

(1) *Constitutional factors* include genetically determined predispositions (for example, to affective disorders or schizophrenia), as well as specific inherited disorders, and conditions due to chromosome abnormalities (see Chapter 2 of my *Basic Child Psychiatry* – see note 5).

(2) *Temperamental factors* are those features of the child's basic temperament (see Chess and Thomas[22]) which are considered important in the case.

(3) *Physical factors* are causative or associated organic disorders and diseases.

(4) *Psychological factors* include the internal mental and emotional life of the child, important aspects of which are the child's cognitive style and abilities.

(5) *Environmental factors* take in the family system and the school environment, and the wider social setting to which the child is exposed.

Protective factors, those that are limiting the severity of the disorder and promoting healthy functioning, are an important part of the formulation. They include the family's strengths and assets as well as the child's.

Construction of the grid (or assembling the information in any

73

Figure 4.2 Formulation grid of contributing factors

	Constitutional	Temperamental	Physical	Psychological	Environmental
Predisposing					
Precipitating					
Perpetuating					
Protective					

other way) is only the first stage in developing the formulation. The next, important, step is setting out what you believe to be the relative importance of the various factors you have identified and how you consider them to be interacting to produce the disorder which the child or the family presents.

The formulation should be a clearly written, logical, dynamic explanation of the case, leading to a plan of treatment, management, or further assessment. Strengths as well as weaknesses should be included. The following, reproduced from my *Basic Child Psychiatry*, is an example of a formulation:

Angela B. presents as a reserved, anxious twelve-year-old girl with a three-year history of reluctance to attend school despite three changes of school arranged by her mother at Angela's insistence. During the last six months her attendance record has been less than 50%. She is a physically fit girl who has just reached puberty. She is said always to have been a quiet child, slow to adapt to change and overdependent on her mother. The latter has long been unable to resist Angela's demands, and behaves similarly towards Angela's nine-year-old sister who seems, however, to have a more assertive personality than Angela and is developing more independence than her sister.

Before the onset of school refusal Angela did well at school and she appears to be of above average intelligence. Non-attendance was precipitated by a change to a stricter, male teacher and a period of illness in mother. Now attempts to get Angela to go to school result in panic and an acute exacerbation of anxiety symptoms. Angela has, however, a keen interest in horses and attends riding school on her own with no difficulty. In this area of her life her self-esteem appears good, but in others it is poor and she feels unable to cope with many situations without the support of others, especially her mother.

Mrs B. and the two daughters have a close, enmeshed relationship; there is a clear boundary between their family subsystem and Mr B., who makes only a small contribution to the upbringing of the children and volunteered little during the family interview. He spent part of his childhood in a group home and seems uninvolved in family life. He has an adequately paid job working in a bank.

The whole family appears to need support over sending

75

Angela to school. At the same time the relationship between the parents requires to be strengthened; boundaries must be established between the parents on the one hand and the two daughters on the other.

Although the problem is a longstanding one, the parents are strongly motivated to receive help and are concerned about the amount of schooling Angela has missed. Mr B. seems willing, even keen, to get more involved in the parenting process but at present lacks the necessary skills or confidence. Other strengths are Angela's good physical health, her above average intelligence and her interests outside the home, notably in horses. With treatment, which will have to address the family system problems as well as being concerned simply with getting Angela back in school, the outlook for improvement is good. Angela may require some individual therapy as well as the family work. If early return to school is not achieved a short period of inpatient treatment may be indicated.

Formulations usually require to be updated from time to time, when children and families are under treatment and as more information becomes available. Few, if any assessments are the last word, and in a sense every diagnostic assessment and formulation should be regarded as provisional. We can never know everything about any person or family.

RECORDING THE ASSESSMENT

Good records are as necessary in child psychiatry as in other branches of medicine. They should be written in concise, economical prose and are best typed. A systematic format, for example one using the headings in this chapter, is much to be desired. Any drawings, paintings, or written material produced by the child should be part of the record.

NOTES

1 S. Minuchin, *Families and Family Therapy*, Cambridge, Mass.: Harvard University Press, 1974.
2 M. A. Karper and E. S. Strauss, *Family Evaluation*, New York: Gardner Press, 1983.
3 R. Bandler, J. Grinder, and V. Satir, *Changing with Families*, Palo Alto: Science and Behaviour Books, 1976.

4 R. Bandler and J. Grindler, *Frogs into Princes*, Moab, Utah: Real People Press, 1979.
5 P. Barker, *Basic Child Psychiatry*, 5th edn, Oxford: Blackwell Scientific; Chicago: Year Book, 1988.
6 P. Barker, *Basic Family Therapy*, 2nd edn, Oxford: Blackwell Scientific; New York: Oxford University Press.
7 J. H. DiLeo, *Interpreting Children's Drawings*, New York: Brunner/ Mazel, 1983.
8 K. J. Zimet and G. K. Farley, 'Four perspectives on the competence and self-esteem of emotionally disturbed children beginning day treatment', *Journal of the American Academy of Child Psychiatry* 24 (1986): 76–83.
9 J. D. Goodman and J. A. Sours, *The Child Mental Status Examination*, New York: Basic Books, 1967.
10 J. E. Simmons, *Psychiatric Examination of Children*, 4th edn, Philadelphia: Lea & Febiger.
11 V. P. Varma, *Anxiety in Children*, London: Croom Helm; New York: Methuen, 1984.
12 P. Barker, 'Recognition and treatment of anxiety in children by means of psychiatric interview', in V. P. Varma (ed.) *Anxiety in Children*, London: Croom Helm, 1984.
13 M. Rutter and P. Graham, 'The reliability and validity of the psychiatric assessment of the child: 1. Interview with the child', *British Journal of Psychiatry* 114 (1968): 563–79.
14 P. Graham and M. Rutter, 'The reliability and validity of the psychiatric assessment of the child: 2. Interview with the parent', *British Journal of Psychiatry* 114 (1968): 581–92.
15 M. Rutter and A. Cox, 'Psychiatric interviewing techniques: I. Methods and measures', *British Journal of Psychiatry* 138 (1981): 273–82.
16 A. Cox, K. Hopkinson, and M. Rutter, 'Psychiatric interviewing techniques: II. Naturalistic study: eliciting factual information', *British Journal of Psychiatry* 138 (1981): 283–91.
17 K. Hopkinson, A. Cox, and M. Rutter, 'Psychiatric interviewing techniques: III. Naturalistic study: eliciting feelings', *British Journal of Psychiatry* 138 (1981): 406–15.
18 M. Rutter, A. Cox, S. Egert, D. Holbrook, and B. Everitt, 'Psychiatric interviewing techniques: IV. Experimental study: four contrasting styles', *British Journal of Psychiatry* 138 (1981): 456–65.
19 A. Cox, M. Rutter, and D. Holbrook, 'Psychiatric interviewing techniques: V. Experimental study: eliciting factual information', *British Journal of Psychiatry* 139 (1981): 29–37.
20 A. Cox, D. Holbrook, and M. Rutter, 'Psychiatric interviewing techniques: VI. Experimental study: eliciting feelings', *British Journal of Psychiatry* 139 (1981): 144–52.
21 H. Aponte, 'The family–school interview: an eco-structural approach', *Family Process* 15 (1976): 303–11.

22 S. Chess and A. Thomas, *Origins and Evolution of Behaviour Disorders From Infancy to Early Adult Life*, New York: Brunner/Mazel, 1984.

Chapter Five

PSYCHOLOGICAL ASSESSMENT AND THE MANAGEMENT OF CHILDREN WITH EMOTIONAL AND BEHAVIOURAL DIFFICULTIES

DAVID JONES

The purpose of this chapter is to help identify the role of psychological assessment in the provision of a theoretical basis for the management of children with emotional and behavioural difficulties. It will not be possible to cover all methods of assessment or to refer to all of the variations of disturbed behaviour which occur in children and adolescents. What becomes immediately obvious on interviewing troubled children and their families or teachers is that there are usually several problems being talked about and that the one which initially precipitated the referral is not necessarily the most important. Childhood disturbances are rarely as clear cut as adult psychiatric disorders and there will often appear to be too many explanations for the child's problem behaviours in the early history, in the current family interactions, or in the child's school experiences.

Modern-day psychological assessment is likely to be able to contribute to the management of emotionally and behaviourally disturbed children by eliciting information in one or more of three ways, depending upon the needs of the situation. First, there may be a need for assessment of both cognitive potential and current level of cognitive functioning and academic attainments. Second, it may be important to obtain quantitative estimates of the child's personality characteristics and of ways the child is perceived by others. These measures can then be related to normative data obtained from large groups of children of the same age. Third, it may be valuable to quantify or analyse the occurrences of the problem symptoms by involving the child together with the family or others in a behavioural assessment.

THE ROLE OF COGNITIVE ASSESSMENT

It has to be recognized that the psychological testing of children has become an increasingly controversial subject in recent years. There have been two major sources of concern. The first has been over the validity of psychological tests. In particular, attention has been focused on the limitations of intelligence testing. Is there really a general capacity for problem solving and learning which can be measured effectively in less than an hour? If so, can it be measured in poorly motivated, disturbed, or withdrawn children? The second concern has been the more general one of a reluctance to apply a medical-disease model to children showing behavioural difficulties when the analysis of the problem should be at the level of functioning of the family or some more complex social system. These concerns have to be taken seriously, not least because they are often voiced by psychologists themselves, even some of the ones who do the testing.

What, then, are the justifications for continuing with psychometric assessments? The most powerful argument is that management of a problem still depends upon having a way of formulating the problem. Different levels of analysis and interpretation are possible and these can often supplement each other. Psychological testing provides information relating to the individual, the child or adolescent, in the system. If the information is not needed at that level it should not be elicited. The cases where providing this level of detail is helpful most often are those in which the children may well have special educational needs. There will be other cases where information about the child has to be channelled into the system to help modify the behaviour of parents or other carers towards the child. Indeed, the behaviour or expectations of the parents may well be the most important subject for a behavioural assessment. The challenge is for the psychologist to gather information as objectively as possible and to be willing to formulate hypotheses to identify or help eliminate areas of difficulty. Nevertheless, it is important that the assessment is not seen as a labelling exercise with the categories of emotional and behavioural difficulties being allowed to slip in as substitutes for the older catch-all category of maladjusted children.

The contribution of careful cognitive assessment, together with the measurement of attainments, to the management of behaviourally difficult children and to the recognition of and provision for their special educational needs, can best be illustrated by a series of examples of practical decision taking. In many cases the assessment will be carried out to help eliminate the presence of a cognitive difficulty or handicap. Feeding information about the child into the management system is as important as the assessment itself. It must be done in a way which is not detrimental to the child. For this reason IQ scores and diagnostic labels will rarely be used but the strengths and weaknesses of the child need to be clearly identified. For reasons of space limitations most of the discussion will be confined to problems in school-age children.

Identification of learning difficulties

In a small but significant number of children, emotionally disturbed behaviour is a secondary feature of undetected learning difficulty. 'Learning difficulty' is the term currently in use to identify those children whose general level of intellectual functioning is of the order of two standard deviations or more below the mean for their age-group. Children with IQs in the range 50–70 are referred to as having Moderate Learning Difficulty. Prior to the 1981 Education Act these children were referred to as Educationally Subnormal in the United Kingdom and as Educable Mental Retardates in the United States. Children with IQs below about 50 on standard tests are now referred to as having Severe Learning Difficulty. It is important that these terms are used correctly in discussions with parents and that learning problems in children of otherwise average or above-average cognitive abilities are referred to as specific learning difficulties.

Severe learning difficulty is likely to have been identified long before the child begins school and hopefully special provision will have started by the nursery stage. Mostly, in addition, moderate learning difficulty will be identified in the pre-school child. In some cases, for whatever reason, the learning difficulty will have gone undetected, occasionally even up until adolescence. These children are exposed to more frequent academic failures than their classmates, which often results in lowered self-esteem. They may react in a variety of ways to their adverse experiences. Not uncommonly the reaction is a conduct disorder involving some degree of acting-out in the school situation. How bad this behaviour has to be before someone suggests that it is unacceptable is largely one of tolerance. The problem of the child who has difficulty in learning has now also become one of containing disruptive behaviour for teachers. The parents may also be struggling with difficult behaviour at home or feeling angry or annoyed because the school is asking them to exert a degree of influence on the child when they feel they cannot understand the problem. Other children with learning difficulty respond to their experiences of failure by becoming increasingly withdrawn and morose. They may start staying away from school for trivial reasons and as a consequence fall even further behind in terms of academic progress. These quiet non-trouble-making children of low ability form one of the most easily overlooked groups of problems.

Whilst concern has been expressed over the possibility of previously undetected learning difficulty, it must be recognized that many behaviourally disturbed children may give a misleading impression of low cognitive ability. Accurate testing of children who might well far rather be doing something else, or who want to make the point that they are not willing to co-operate with anyone, is not always possible. For this reason the results of a group test of intelligence will rarely be satisfactory for these children. Even in individual testing it can take time to establish rapport and more than one session may be necessary. One of the biggest problems is assessing the child who is negative and gives up at the first sign of difficulty or the need for effort. This behaviour may be one of the last resorts the child may have for preserving self-esteem and avoiding further public experience of failure. It is sad to have to recognize that much of the present antagonism to testing arises from past incorrect labelling of difficult children as Educationally Subnormal because they obtained low scores on intelligence tests partly through poor co-operation and indifference to the occasion. Psychologists have to be more prepared than in the past to acknowledge when they have failed to obtain a reliable estimate of a child's ability. The presence of learning difficulty can often be excluded after only a few minutes of testing. More typically, with school-age children about eight or nine subtests of the WISC-R[1] or a range of tests from the British Abilities Scales[2] will provide a sufficiently wide profile to allow an accurate estimate of ability level.

Identification of learning difficulty is only one small step towards effective management. For many parents this is the last thing they want to find out about their children. Only careful explanation will help them understand that the child has special needs and will not achieve his or her potential unless these needs are adequately met. The professional will also be aware that lack of resources may well mean that there will still be a considerable delay before any extra provision will be possible. On the part of the school there may well be defensiveness because the problems were not identified earlier. Certainly the provision of good learning support services within the mainstream school will often alleviate the need for preparing the child for a change of school.

Recognizing specific learning difficulties

Quite frequently children with behavioural and emotional difficulties will be reported to be underachieving in one or more areas of academic performance even though they appear to be at least within the average range in general ability. Usually the problem is one of reading difficulty although backwardness in number skills may sometimes be the case. Few conditions arouse such emotion among parents and professionals alike as reading difficulty. DSM-III, which is the major current medical classification system of the American Psychiatric Association,[3] includes reading difficulty in children as a developmental disorder but there have been strong objections to its inclusion in the system. The use of the diagnostic label of dyslexia, or more properly developmental dyslexia, still arouses controversy. Certainly many psychologists, physicians, speech therapists, and educators use the term and many parents almost prize it as an explanatory concept for reading failure. Equally firmly, many teachers and psychologists prefer to say that there are some children who for a variety of reasons have failed to learn to read and who are in need of remedial support. It would be beyond the scope of this chapter to attempt to resolve the theoretical differences between these positions. What is important for the management of the child is to try to resolve uncertainty over whether the behavioural difficulties are largely a consequence of the specific learning difficulty. Certainly, not all children with learning handicaps show disturbed behaviour, but not infrequently feelings of failure and frustration result in some degree of rebelliousness, anger, or bewilderment.

The need for a careful assessment of the specific learning difficulties becomes even more apparent when it is recognized that many children with emotional difficulties will be underachieving at school as a consequence of their poor motivation and inadequate co-operation. Superficial comparison of the results of attainment tests will not distinguish between this latter group of emotionally disturbed underachieving children and those whose underachievement is mainly a result of specific learning difficulties. Yet the two groups have very different educational and remedial needs. Even using simple screening tests of reading accuracy such as the Schonell Graded Word Reading Test[4] or the reading test of the British Abilities Scales (see note 2), it is possible to recognize some of the more obvious phonemic difficulties. The Neale Analysis of Reading Ability[5] provides estimates of reading speed, accuracy, and comprehension and allows a more detailed analysis of errors and substitutions. For the analysis of spelling the Schonell Graded Word Spelling Test (see note 4), remains one of the most frequently used tests. Recent developments in cognitive neuropsychology have provided insight into the acquisition of reading skills in normal children as well as those with reading difficulties. From this work has come such techniques as comparing the ability to read regular and irregular words and non-words.

Children with specific learning difficulty will often co-operate despite repeated past failures if they feel that the nature of their difficulties has been understood. Unfortunately, designing remedial programmes is only the first stage of an intensive process which requires more resources than the system is often able to provide. With adolescents it is sometimes possible to give them strategies for reducing the impact of the difficulties on their career prospects or to make them aware of different ways of continuing their education after reaching school-leaving age. The underachievers without serious learning difficulties are unlikely to respond to remedial instruction without further efforts to improve their motivation as part of the therapeutic effort to reduce their emotional distress.

Failing to meet parents' expectations

Another situation in which there are strong indications for an assessment of intellectual ability is when the referring problem is one of emotionally disturbed behaviour, together with complaints that the child is underachieving or has recently failed the selection tests for entry to a new school. This sort of referral is not infrequently initiated by the family doctor, who has been consulted by the parents. Typically these will be middle-class or professional parents who have high expectations of their children. On testing these children are often found to be of Average or High Average ability with no indications of specific learning difficulties, but they are failing in terms of the demands placed upon them. They will often either be attending or making applications to selective private schools where competition for entry has resulted in average IQ levels of well above 120. The experiences of failure in this sort of situation can be every bit as severe as those of children with undetected learning difficulty. Once motivation is affected the child will sometimes make things worse by virtually giving up trying in the competitive environment.

The ability profile of these 'over-educated' children is typically a well-developed vocabulary relative to other test results. Also, the Verbal IQ tends to be a little higher than the Performance IQ, with the lowest scores being on the more culture-fair tests. It is not an easy task to modify the expectations of parents who may well feel that an IQ of, say, 112 is a failure in their child. Even more difficult may be the problem of choice of school and reconciling the parents to the local comprehensive as the best available option for the child.

Hyperactive syndrome and minimal dysfunction conditions

One of the most common complaints about emotionally and behaviourally disturbed children is that they are hyperactive, fidgety, easily distractible, unable to concentrate, and sometimes also that they are clumsy. Just what this means is a function of who has been asked to report on the child. There seems to be a greater tendency to apply the clinical label hyperactive or hyperkinetic in the United States than in Britain. In some large-scale surveys, up to a third of children have been described as overactive and distractible by either their parents or their teachers. A study of 10 and 11 year-olds on the Isle of Wight by Schacher et al.[6] reported that teachers rated 9.9 per cent of these children as hyperactive and parents rated 8.3 per cent of the children as hyperactive. However, only 2.2 per cent of the children were given hyperactivity ratings by both parents and teachers. The children in this latter group were referred to as pervasively hyperactive and appeared to have lower scores on cognitive tests and to be more likely to show conduct disorders than those rated as hyperactive by either parents or teachers, who were referred to as situationally hyperactive. Although this distinction is superficial it underlines the importance of obtaining ratings from both parents and teachers. Where the behaviour problem is limited to specific situations such as the home, then the initial approach to management can be structured in that environment.

Hyperactivity is only a problem if it upsets others or interferes with the child's capacity to learn. It is reported as occurring more frequently in boys than in girls. Many parents and some teachers find it difficult to accept. It is rarely an isolated behaviour problem and much has been written on whether or not hyperactivity is part of a clinical syndrome. DSM-III (see note 3) proposes the term Attention Deficit Disorder (ADD) to identify children who display developmentally inappropriate inattention, impulsivity, and hyper-activity. The diagnosis is only applied to children who show the symptoms before the age of 7 to distinguish the condition from emotionally disturbed behaviour and conduct disorders which develop as a result of specific learning difficulties or problems at school. Barkley[7] takes a similar position but suggests that the onset should be before the age of 6. Certainly, when inattention, impulsiv-ity, and hyperactivity occur together the child is likely to irritate others and have difficulty both in concentrating and in conforming in the conventional classroom environment. An exceedingly difficult question to answer is whether the child's difficulties in this case are consequential on some form of neurological immaturity or a reaction to adverse environmental experiences. At the risk of complicating the position even further it has to be recognized that the emotionally disturbed behaviours of these children might be another direct symptom of the constitutional immaturity or a reaction to the feel-ings of anger, unfairness or inadequacy experienced by ADD chil-dren in their struggles with parental authority and experiences of not fitting in at school.

Psychological testing of these children is not an easy task although some of them will give good initial co-operation in a one-to-one situation. Proportionally, hyperactivity and the related attention problems occur more frequently in children who are in the learning difficulty range in cognitive abilities, but the problems also occur in children of average or above-average ability. Educational man-agement will be guided by the pattern of abilities and the degree of underachievement by the time of referral. Both attention capacity and impulsivity as behavioural characteristics can be measured but they will often be found to be situation-specific. Some authorities suggest that these children may have a disorder of the arousal system and that the distractibility is a consequence of their being underaroused and seeking stimulation. Testing will often show that their performance is a function of motivation. This observation does more than just change the name of the construct because it draws attention to the need to identify the reinforcement hierarchies of the individual. Parents may then be helped to be more consistent and more aware in their administration of rewards and punishments. The defining of boundaries in family-therapy terminology can also be facilitated if parents are enabled to understand this information.

Returning to the patterns of ability typically elicited on the assessment of children referred as hyperactive, it quickly becomes apparent that this is a heterogeneous group. In the past such terms as minimal brain damage and minimal cerebral dysfunction were used almost synonymously with hyperactivity on the assumption that the behavioural disturbances were a consequence of organic damage even though demonstrable signs of neurological impairment were absent. However, since many children with known brain damage do not show symptoms of hyperactivity, the validity of the minimal brain damage diagnosis is in doubt.[8] What some of these children do show on testing are minor difficulties on complex perceptual or visuo-constructional tasks. Others might show impairment in responding to figure-ground relationships or in visual memory tasks. Tests such as the Frostig Developmental Test of Visual Perception[9] and the Benton Revised Visual Retention Test[10] provide useful supplementary information on these impairments.

Another problem area for some children is the development of motor skills. Some workers refer to the clumsy child syndrome[11] to describe the slightly uncoordinated, distractible child who again may not show any clear signs of organic impairment apart from soft neurological signs like minor asymmetries in reflexes or small irregularities in electroencephalograms. Children with these problems are at risk in the sense that they may be teased or ignored because of their poor performance at games. They may be the victims of bullying. Even those who are of high intelligence may need vocational guidance so that they may concentrate on subjects which will not be influenced by their indifferent performance on motor skills. It is also important that these children should not be labelled as failures at school and that they should be given the opportunities to play less competitive sports than the traditional team games.

Much has been written on possible links between left-handedness and specific learning difficulties. Once again there is a partial rejection of the older viewpoint. Left-handers with firmly established hand preference seem to do as well as right-handers, but the children with poorly established hand preference who are not particularly skilled with either hand seem to be more likely to have a range of other problems.

The overlap between hyperactivity, aggressive behaviour, and conduct disturbances comes up time and time again. Certainly many children show complex and multiple forms of disturbed behaviour. Research and clinical evidence indicates that hyperactive behaviour sometimes occurs without evidence of aggressive behaviour.

ASSESSMENT OF PERSONALITY CHARACTERISTICS

Recent psychiatric classification systems of children's disorders such as the World Health Organization System[12] and the American Psychiatric Association's DSM-III (see note 3) have adopted multiaxial classifications which still rely on a medical model of disease categories. Using psychological tests to identify personality characteristics provides a methodology for increasing the validity of some of the psychiatric categories, but in this context testing is at best making a superficial contribution to the management of behavioural difficulties. A more widely adopted approach to classification has been to focus on groups of symptoms or descriptions of behaviour characteristics provided by parents, teachers, and others. What has emerged with surprising consistency from a number of studies is a division of children's difficulties into emotional or neurotic problems as one cluster and conduct problems as a second cluster. Achenbach,[13, 14] for example, using a factor-analytic method, identified two factors which he referred to as *internalizing* and *externalizing*. The internalizing cluster includes withdrawn, anxious, and inhibited behaviours and symptoms such as phobias, sleep disturbances, and general aches and pains. The externalizing cluster includes antisocial, delinquent, and aggressive behaviours with specific problems like stealing and vandalism. A similar dichotomy has been identified by the Rutter 'Children's Behaviour Questionnaire for Completion by Teachers' which has been used widely for screening large groups of children for behaviour difficulties in Britain.[15] The Rutter Scale first identifies children who have a high number of reported problem behaviours and then provides scores on neurotic and antisocial subscales.

Allocating children to one or other of these two broad categories of disturbance may appear to oversimplify the complexity of the wide range of individual differences seen in children. Nevertheless it can be a valuable first step in the decision process on which, if any, personality tests should be administered. A few examples will be given of the sorts of tests used to provide a personality profile of the child. In the space available the selection has to be limited.

One of the most widely measured of all personality characteristics in children is anxiety.[16] Most measures are in the form of self-report questionnaires or check-lists to be completed by the child and give an estimate of trait anxiety or the degree of anxiety proneness. The Neuroticism Scale of the Junior Eysenck Personality Inventory[17] provides a typical means of estimating general anxiety level and can be useful in identifying children who might be well above the mean for their age-group. An alternative test which is a little easier to use with younger children and has normative data for the 5–12 years age-group is the Child Anxiety Scale.[18] The Spielberger State-Trait Anxiety Inventory for Children[19] has the advantage of also measuring state anxiety, the 'how I feel now' response to a series of statements. Measures of state anxiety can provide a useful, quick method for monitoring changes in the highly anxious child as a function of response to therapy. An estimate of anxiety level is often useful when decisions need to be taken on the management of school refusers. Recent improvements and wider applications of relaxation techniques have made anxiety management by behavioural means a more readily available method of intervention. Very high scores on anxiety measures indicate the need for caution in interpreting the results of cognitive tests.

For those wanting more ambitious measuring instruments providing estimates on multiple personality-characteristics the choice is either to administer a lengthy questionnaire to the child or to the parents. The Children's Personality Questionnaire[20] is a children's version of the 16PF and provides scores on fourteen dimensions, one of which is intelligence for children aged between 8 and 12 years. The items are in a forced-choice form so the child has to choose between two alternatives, for example 'Do you have many friends or just a few good friends?' Examples of the source traits are Self-assured vs. Apprehensive, Affected by Feelings vs. Emotionally Stable, and Shy vs. Venturesome. It is also possible to obtain scores on the two higher-order factors of anxiety and extraversion derived from the source traits. One major problem is that the questionnaire can take up to 50 minutes for the child to complete and not all disturbed children are willing to give that amount of co-operation. A version suitable for younger children is the Early School Personality Questionnaire.[21] This measures thirteen primary source-traits and has normative data for children aged 6–8 years. Adolescents can be given the Junior–Senior High School Personality Questionnaire.[22] The Personality Inventory for Children[23] consists of 600 items to be completed by the parent and yields scores on fourteen clinical subscales such as Defensiveness, Withdrawal, Anxiety, and Social Skills. The inventory is essentially a downward extension of the Minnesota Multiphasic Personality Inventory (MMPI) and has a manual for interpreting profiles.

An important personality characteristic which is receiving increased attention in terms of attempts at measurement is childhood depression. The Children's Depression Scale[24] is a sixty-six item self-report scale suitable for use with the age range 9–16 years. An alternative measure of depression is the Children's Depression Inventory[25] which has been derived from the well-known Beck Depression Scale. Indications of depressed behaviour can also be obtained from careful observation of children during cognitive assessment. It is worth recording that although consideration of assessing depression is usually given to anxious, withdrawn, and lethargic children, depression can be a serious problem in conduct-disorder children who display antisocial behaviour.

BEHAVIOURAL ASSESSMENT

The behavioural assessment is qualitatively different from the traditional psychiatric interview. The initial interview with the family seeks information about the child's problem behaviours and focuses on what happens before these behaviours occur. It also concentrates on what happens afterwards that might be reinforcing or maintaining these behaviours. This information may have to be gathered in stages. Sometimes the parents will need to be trained to make and record observations. The procedure has to be flexible and the psychologist may also want to observe the child at home or at school. The problem behaviours are identified as targets and base-line estimates of frequency are assembled. The approach may be different for temper outbursts, bed-wetting, self-mutilation, subst-ance abuse, or phobic responses, but the emphasis on careful obser-vation and quantification of the problem is the same. It often requires considerable insight and experience to identify the preced-ing events, or antecedent stimuli, which signal to the child the likelihood that the disturbed behaviour will attain reinforcement. In addition, the nature of the reinforcement to the child may not be readily discernible. Especially when the problem behaviour is the product of complex interactions within the family, it is appropri-ate that all of the family members should be involved in trying to define it and in recognizing how they respond after the event.

Whilst the behavioural assessment would normally be part of a therapeutic intervention based on a learning theory or cognitive–behavioural approach, it can be adapted to provide quantitative data for the evaluation of therapeutic change when other treatment models are being used. Sometimes it is appropriate to extend the assessment process by inviting parents, siblings, class-mates, or teachers of the child to complete rating scales on the child's behav-iour. The following examples give some idea of the sort of instru-ments available for these purposes.

Rating scales completed by parents

The Parent Symptom Questionnaire[26] developed by Conners is one of the most frequently used instruments for recording parents' opinions on their children. The commonly used version of the scale has forty-eight items and gives scores on conduct problems, learning disability (inattention), psychosomatic problems, impulsivity–hyperactivity, and anxiety. There are US norms for children aged from 3–17 years. Minor modifications of the wording are advisable for British use. The number of items contributing to each score is relatively small but it has been found that high overall scores are often associated with poor academic performance. Inspection of response patterns often provides valuable insights into situational difficulties.

A modified form of the Werry–Weiss–Peters Activity Rating Scale[27] provides a brief survey of the child's behaviour across seven settings: meals, television, homework, play, sleep, public places, and school. Other specific items could be added to the scale to cover the differing life-styles of some families. Scales of this sort are good at spotting non-compliance to parents' commands and also as measures of situational hyperactivity.

A final example is the Child Behaviour Check List, which is one of a series of instruments developed by Achenbach.[28] This provides scores on a number of syndromes such as Aggressive, Delinquent, and Uncommunicative.

Rating scales completed by teachers

Rutter's Children's Behaviour Questionnaire for Completion by Teachers (see note 15) was referred to above and is an extremely useful report on aspects of the child's behaviour which most teachers are willing to complete. The Conners Teacher Rating Scale is another widely used checklist on which children are rated on group participation, classroom behaviour, and attitude towards authority (see note 26). Among other things it provides an estimate of hyperactivity in the classroom.

A final example of teacher rating scales is the Bristol Social-Adjustment Guides[29] developed by Stott. Analysis of responses produces measures on five core syndromes: Unforthcomingness, Withdrawal, Depression, Inconsequence, and Hostility. Measures of this sort can be used for initial assessment and to monitor the effects of intervention.

CONCLUDING REMARKS

In the final analysis the question of how detailed a psychological assessment should be is a complex value judgement which should be based on whether the information obtained will help guide the management of the child. Excluding difficulties can often be as important as identifying them. This brief review has not been able to focus on the assessment of language difficulties. Neither has it been able to discuss the behavioural difficulties sometimes seen in children with neurological impairment or epilepsy. Each of these conditions requires a detailed cognitive assessment and a behavioural assessment to identify the child's special needs. There is always the need to be vigilant when assessing behaviourally disturbed children. Mild difficulties in comprehension or constructional ability may be the only detectable signs of organic involvement. Thus, for example, when problems of this sort occur in a child who is also reported to have uncontrollable outbursts of aggression, there is a need to exclude temporal lobe epilepsy. Again, the assessment and management of autistic and psychotic children has not been discussed. These children have considerable special needs and merit separate attention.

Of the various forms of frequently occurring emotionally disturbed behaviour, conduct disorders bring the child into sharpest conflict with others. Children with these problems are often the most difficult to treat and the most difficult to engage in effective intervention programmes. They have attracted so much attention because of the problems they cause in schools. It has been argued that assessment will sometimes identify special educational needs in these children which will have to be met in addition to attempting to modify the behaviour disturbances. The behavioural difficulties themselves are best likely to be managed following an individually designed behavioural analysis, supplemented where necessary by the use of personality measures or rating scales completed by parents or teachers.

NOTES

1 D. Wechsler, *Wechsler Intelligence Scale for Children – Revised*, New York: The Psychological Corporation, 1974.
2 C. Elliott, D. J. Murray, and L. S. Pearson, *British Ability Scales – Revised*, Windsor: NFER-Nelson, 1983.
3 American Psychiatric Association, *Diagnostic and Statistical Manual of Mental Disorders*, 3rd Edn, Washington, DC, 1980.
4 F. J. Schonell, *Reading and Spelling Tests*, Edinburgh: Oliver & Boyd, 1955.
5 M. D. Neale, *Neale Analysis of Reading Ability Manual*, London: Macmillan, 1958.
6 M. Schacher, M. Rutter, and A. Smith, 'The characteristics of situationally and pervasively hyperactive children', *Journal of Child Psychology and Psychiatry* 20 (1981): 375–92.

7 R. A. Barkley, *Hyperactive Children: A Handbook for Diagnosis and Treatment*, Chichester: Wiley, 1981.
8 M. Rutter, 'Brain damage syndromes in childhood: concepts and findings', *Journal of Child Psychology and Psychiatry* 18 (1977): 1–21.
9 M. Frostig, *Developmental Test of Visual Perception*, Palo Alto: Consulting Psychologists Press, 1966.
10 A. L. Benton, *Revised Visual Retention Test*, New York: The Psychological Corporation, 1974.
11 S. E. Henderson, 'The assessment of clumsy children: old and new approaches', *Journal of Child Psychology and Psychiatry* 28 (1987): 511–27.
12 M. Rutter, 'Classification', in M. Rutter and L. Hersov (eds) *Child Psychiatry: Modern Approaches* Oxford: Blackwell, 1977, pp. 359–84.
13 T. M. Achenbach, 'The classification of children's psychiatric symptoms', *Psychological Monographs* 80 (Whole no. 615) (1966): 1–37.
14 T. M. Achenbach, 'The child behavior profile: an empirically based system for assessing children's behavioral problems and competencies', *International Journal of Mental Health* 1 (1979): 24–42.
15 M. Rutter, 'A children's behaviour questionnaire', *Journal of Child Psychiatry and Psychology* 8 (1967): 1–11.
16 D. Jones, 'Recognition of anxiety by psychometric tests', in V. P. Varma (ed.) *Anxiety in Children*, London: Croom Helm, 1984, pp. 15–34.
17 S. B. G. Eysenck, *Manual of the Junior Eysenck Personality Inventory*, London: University of London Press, 1965.
18 J. S. Gillis, *Child Anxiety Scale Manual*, Champaign, Illinois: Institute for Personality and Ability Testing, 1980.
19 C. D. Spielberger, D. C. Edwards, J. Montouri, and R. E. Lushene, *The State-Trait Anxiety Inventory for Children*, Palo Alto: Consulting Psychologists Press, 1970.
20 R. B. Porter and R. B. Cattell, *The Children's Personality Questionnaire*, Champaign, Illinois: Institute for Personality and Ability Testing, 1963.
21 R. W. Coan and R. B. Cattell, *Early School Personality Questionnaire*, Champaign, Illinois: Institute for Personality and Ability Testing, 1966.
22 R. B. Cattell, *The Junior–Senior High School Personality Questionnaire*, Champaign, Illinois: Institute for Personality and Ability Testing, 1965.
23 R. D. Wirt, D. Lacher, J. K. Klinedinst, and P. D. Seat, *Multidimensional Description of Child Personality: A Manual for the Personality Inventory for Children*, Los Angeles: Western Psychological Services, 1977.
24 M. Lang and M. Tisher, *Children's Depression Scale*, Victoria: Australian Council for Educational Research, 1978.
25 M. Kovacs, 'Rating scales to assess depression in school-aged children', *Acta Paedopsychiatrica* 46 (1981): 305–15.
26 C. H. Goyette, C. K. Conners, and R. F. Ulrich, 'Normative data on

revised Conners parent and teachers rating scales', *Journal of Abnormal Child Psychology* 6 (1978): 221–36.

27 D. K. Routh, C. S. Schroeder, and L. O'Tuama, 'Development of activity level in children', *Developmental Psychology* 10 (1974): 163–68.

28 T. M. Achenbach, *Assessment and Taxonomy of Child and Adolescent Psychopathology*, Beverly Hills: Sage, 1985.

29 D. H. Stott, *The Social Adjustment of Children: Manual of the Bristol Social-Adjustment Guides*, London: Hodder & Stoughton, 1974.

Chapter Six

THE PSYCHOANALYTIC PSYCHOTHERAPY OF CHILDREN WITH EMOTIONAL AND BEHAVIOURAL DIFFICULTIES

F. M. J. DALE

INTRODUCTION

Although it is important to distinguish the aims and methods of psychoanalytic psychotherapy from other psychotherapeutic approaches, it will not be our intention to suggest that, *regardless of circumstances*, it can or should always be the preferred method of treatment offered to the troubled child or family. The aim will be to define those areas in which psychoanalytic psychotherapy is the most appropriate therapeutic intervention, as well as indicating how psychoanalytic concepts and practices can be useful as an adjunct to other ways of working with disturbed children.

Almost without exception, the psychoanalytic treatment of children is made possible, and takes place, within a multidisciplinary framework in which close co-operation between involved professionals is often the crucial factor in providing the appropriate setting and network support to enable therapy to proceed with a reasonable chance of success.[1]

PSYCHOANALYTIC PSYCHOTHERAPY AS A METHOD OF TREATMENT

Historically, psychoanalytic psychotherapy[2] with children derives from Freud's discovery and elucidation of unconscious processes and the mechanisms of splitting, denial, projection, displacement, and regression (amongst others) as defensive methods employed by disturbed adults in order to protect themselves from distressing or unbearable experiences with which they cannot cope. Subsequently, Freud's ideas were taken up, incorporated, and modified by child analysts whose primary concern was the treatment of children with severe emotional and/or behavioural disturbances.

As a result of the clinical experiences of such pioneers as Margaret Lowenfeld, Anna Freud, and Melanie Klein, the basic precepts and methods of psychoanalytic work with adults became modified in order to meet both the specific requirements of professionals who chose to apply the psychoanalytic method to their work with children, and the needs of the children themselves.

With adult patients, even though they may have ambivalent feelings about engaging in the analytic relationship, it is usually assumed that they will be sufficiently motivated to bring themselves along for therapy and at least to attempt to adhere to the 'rules' of analysis: to say what they are thinking or feeling (i.e. free association), not to miss sessions or to walk out before time, and not to displace impulses or feelings aroused in the analytic context outside that setting (i.e. 'acting out').

In the case of children, however, the above conditions may frequently not be complied with or may not even be relevant. In the first instance, children are not generally held to be personally responsible for their mental or emotional well-being and cannot therefore be expected to be motivated to ask for help or necessarily to accept it when offered. It is their parents or legal guardian who must do this for them and take responsibility for the child receiving the help that he or she requires.

Second, in any relationship with an adult where powerful, frequently frightening, even terrifying emotions are aroused, children are often left with no option but to 'act them out'. Finally, one needs to understand that children – especially in the pre-school years – have a limited capacity to understand verbal instructions or to concentrate on tasks for any length of time which require thinking rather than action.

Modifications in technique

Just as adults naturally express their thoughts and feelings with words, the younger child does this through play and other means of symbolic communication such as painting or drawing. Consequently, psychotherapy with children has come to rely on therapeutic techniques which depend to a large extent on the therapist's ability to understand and to facilitate the non-verbal communications of the child patient.

In order to facilitate this, the child is typically provided with a relatively standard set of materials which can be used in different ways to express his or her current preoccupations: drawing paper and coloured pencils, plasticine, a set of family dolls, sets of farm-yard animals, some wild animals – lion, gorilla, crocodile, elephant, and tortoise, building bricks, a tea-set, and some small cars such as an ambulance, fire-engine, police car, and dust lorry.

The setting

Apart from the relationship with the therapist (which we will examine shortly), the context or setting within which therapy takes place is of prime importance. To facilitate the child's engaging with the therapist and revealing his or her innermost thoughts and feelings, a safe, protected therapeutic environment is essential. This means always meeting in the same room, at the same time of day, and at regular intervals. There should be no extraneous intrusions such as telephone calls or other interruptions and the contents of the room should be as neutral as possible.[3]

PSYCHOANALYTIC PSYCHOTHERAPY AS A TREATMENT CHOICE

When readers are confronted with the plethora of therapeutic treatments available today, they are entitled to ask what it is that makes the psychoanalytic method of treating disturbed children different from other approaches and to know when it is appropriate to employ it in preference to other forms of therapeutic intervention.

While it can be argued that most disturbed children would benefit from a period of psychotherapy, it is the author's view that it should not be offered before the potential resources in the family or caring network which may be mobilized to help the child have been fully explored. This may mean meeting with some, or all family members (or care-workers) in order to establish the extent to which it is the *patterns of family interaction themselves* which constitute the problem, and if so, whether the family structure (i.e. the ways in which the family members typically relate to each other) is flexible enough to make the changes necessary in order to help the identified patient. There are many reasons why this may not be possible.

Criteria for treatment

In many cases, children referred for psychotherapy have no family or relatives who can offer support. Into this category we can include children abandoned as babies, children received into residential or foster care[4] and children who are orphaned.

There is an increasing body of evidence – from child psychotherapists and child psychoanalysts – that even the most chaotic and severely disturbed children can benefit from psychotherapy[5] (always providing that the child's therapy is actively supported by the child's care-workers and that good communications exist between all the professionals involved).

In other instances, parents, while taking adequate care of their child's physical needs, may be unable or unwilling to respond to the need to be loved and cherished. These children may be said to be 'psychically' or emotionally abandoned. One common reason for this is the tendency for all of us to deal (or rather, not to deal) with our own unwanted emotions and impulses by projecting (unconsciously attributing) them to someone else.

The cycle of deprivation

It is, I think, significant that many parents of emotionally disturbed children, have themselves been the victims of some form of abuse in their childhood. When they in turn become parents, these long-forgotten memories, and the unbearable emotions associated with them – fear, hate, anger – which may have been successfully repressed since childhood,[6] may come flooding to the surface when they are confronted as a parent by a demanding or fretful child. In such circumstances, the 'abused child' – now having become a parent – experiences the demands of his or her 'child in reality' as expressing all the rage, fear, sadness which he or she could not own as a child.

Many such parents, when confronted by these 'replica situations' which mirror their own infantile experience, come to relate to their children as a kind of persecuting presence from the past and are driven into identifying both with their children and the abusing parents at the same time. In identifying with the demands or distress

99

of their 'real' children, they are once again threatened with coming face to face with still unresolved issues from the 'child inside them'; whilst in identifying with their parents, they feel as adults, unjustly accused and blamed by their children's behaviour. The following example illustrates this process, as does the case of David which will be referred to later.

> The mother of a 13-month-old boy became so distraught over what she described as his 'hyperactive' behaviour that she was close to having a nervous breakdown. The staff on the paediatric ward to which she was referred were so concerned at her mental and emotional state that they offered to admit the boy on an in-patient basis – although not really satisfied themselves that he was in fact as out of control and overactive as described by his mother.
>
> As a matter of course – in addition to ascertaining the current pattern of relationships existing between the various members of the family – a detailed history was taken of both parents' backgrounds. The following facts emerged. At exactly the age that her son was currently (i.e. 13 months) this mother had been 'given away' by her mother into the care of her grandmother. Although her grandmother had given her 'good enough'[7] mothering, she had never gotten over the original trauma of being given away or been able to forgive her parents for abandoning her. For over 30 years, until *she* became a mother and had her own child, these feelings (of rage, impotence, panic, of falling apart) lay hidden and dormant.
>
> At the precise point that her 'actual child' most exactly mirrored the circumstances surrounding her own abandonment, all the feelings and memories associated with it, but until now shut away, came flooding back with overwhelming force.

As mentioned above, as a 'parent' she experienced her child's demands as unbearably persecuting and unreasonable. She felt inadequate, not 'good enough', and yet at the same time consumed with feelings of guilt at her failure to cope. Her greatest fear was that if he 'didn't improve', or we were not able to help her, that she would have to reject him.

One can see here how she is in identification both with the mother who rejected her, *and* with the child who was rejected. In her identification with the *child*, she is terrified of abandoning him, of not being a good mother, of falling apart. (At times, she did seem to be about to 'fall apart' and one can speculate that this is a re-enactment of emotions which, as a 13-month-old infant, she experi-enced as catastrophic, disintegrative, and unprocessable.) She is also 'punishing herself' (i.e. psychically her mother) in experiencing herself as an inadequate parent. In her identification with the *mother*, she feels threatened, attacked, persecuted, humiliated, and enraged by this 'monster' child. Like her own mother, she feels driven into rejecting her child and into repeating exactly what had happened to her.

The point being made here is not just about how issues which are not resolved at source become re-enacted at a later date and with another person (transgenerational re-enactment),[8] but that if one is able to intervene early enough in this cycle, there is a better chance of preventing this cycle of the projection of psychic trauma from parent to child before it becomes chronic and endemic. In the above case, the mother gained enough insight to be able to withdraw her negative projections from her child, freeing him from the burden of having to express feelings which belonged to an earlier generation and between *another* mother and child. He was allowed to become himself and to own *his* emotions, thoughts, and impulses instead of having to express them for his mother. She, in her turn, began to experience him in a different way. He was 'wonderful', 'a delight to have around', and no longer 'hyperactive and out of control'. We can see here, that the mother's ability to gain some insight into her unconscious relationship to her child was an important factor in deciding whether it was the child, the family, or the individual parent who needed psychotherapeutic help.

All too often, however, families with such disturbed patterns of interaction do not come to the attention of the caring services until they move from the private domain of the family into the public domain of nursery, school, or Child Guidance Clinic. At this point, the child's responses to abnormal family patterns may be of such long-standing nature that the child's symptomatic behaviour has changed from being a functional defensive reaction to a threatening or disturbing situation, to an habitual, and increasingly, dysfunc-tional response which has become firmly embedded in the child's character structure and his or her ways of relating to self and other. The *child's* behaviour and interpersonal relationships have now become the problem, and it has moved from being solely a family problem to being one in which individual psychotherapy may be required in order to bring about the necessary *internal changes* which are feeding and maintaining the child's symptomatic behaviour.

Assessing the individual child

Given that the family's – or other caring agency's – resources have been fully explored and found wanting, we are still left with the problem of deciding whether *this* particular child would usefully benefit from psychoanalytic treatment. Any decision must be informed by two sets of criteria: the child's internal resources on the one hand, and on the other the commitment of parents or care-workers in supporting the child's therapy.

The child's internal resources

It is the view of most child psychotherapists that the only way to assess the appropriateness of taking a child into therapy is by way of assessing the child within a 'therapeutic relationship' (what this entails will be gone into in more detail below). This is because *the way in which the child relates* (or fails to relate) to the therapist is frequently a powerful indication of the child's ability to make use of therapy. The child has to be able to 'engage'[9] (at a conscious or unconscious level) with the therapist in order for work to begin. The *manner* in which a child relates to the therapist provides him or her with clues about both its current ways of relating to people but also, perhaps more importantly, about much earlier modes of relating. Two examples from children who underwent therapy should illustrate this.

> Daryl was three and a half years of age when he was referred for therapy. At the time of the referral, he was being cared for by his grandmother – and had been from the age of 18 months at which time his mother returned to the West Indies to pursue her career as a lecturer (it is interesting to note that *his* mother had also been placed with relatives at the same age as Daryl when her mother – Daryl's current grandmother – had left the West Indies to come to England).[10]
> He was referred because of his very demanding, possessive,

and controlling behaviour – particularly towards his grandmother. His behaviour was regressive and infantile; he was still in nappies and would not use the toilet, he had screaming tantrums in which he would bite and scratch at his grandmother if she refused him anything; he had no speech, appeared oblivious to verbal instructions, and seemed to live almost completely in a world of his own.

He was seen by a child psychotherapist and diagnosed as suffering from Autism – a condition in which children withdraw inside themselves, become unreachable, and often exhibit endlessly repetitive, bizarre, and robotic-like movements of hands and body.

In the very first session, I had the impression that this child was not 'there' in the room with me. He was present in body but emotionally and mentally, he was absent. It soon became clear that, in order to make contact with him, to 'engage' him, *I* had to change radically the way in which I would normally interrelate with a child in therapy. Interpreting his behaviour was not enough. One had to somehow find a way of interpreting or relating to his 'internal experience' in order to make any sort of meaningful contact.

Relating to someone's internal experience is part of the expected repertoire of the therapist and is variously called: 'trial identification' or empathy (metaphorically: 'getting inside someone else's skin'). However, with patients whose personality structures are fragmented or which have not been properly integrated in the first place, this can pose serious problems for the therapist who also needs to retain his or her own sense of separateness.

With Daryl, I often felt 'taken over' by him to the extent that I became temporarily dispossessed of my ordinary awareness of myself as 'me' and of having a separate identity.

As one might suspect, the positive indicators in such a case are not good. It took many weeks before Daryl began to engage in therapy, and then only at the level of relating to me as an object,[11] or thing, rather than as a person.

If Daryl related to people as objects or as an extension of himself which he omnipotently controlled through phantasy, Paul, who had been abandoned as a baby but later adopted, related to his therapist as though he were the mother who had originally deserted him.

For years he treated his therapist with contempt and cynicism, denigrating and ridiculing both the therapist and his interpretations. If one were to only take account of his overt behaviour one might have been inclined not to take this boy on in therapy. There would appear to be too many negative indications: the contempt for the therapist, the denial and rejection of any need for help, and the apparent lack of motivation.

However, the therapist, in deciding on whether a particular child will benefit from therapy, also takes into account the child's 'unconscious' motivations. By definition, these will not be accessible to the child at a conscious level. Paul, for example, gave his therapist many indications that despite his apparent indifference, he desperately needed help and wanted therapy to continue. Because of his past disappointments (his adoptive parents had separated just prior to his having therapy), he had learned to protect himself from being let down again by not trusting people. At a conscious level, he could not 'own' his despair, vulnerability, and desire for help. He needed his therapist to 'contain'[12] or hold these emotions for him. After much testing of the therapist's trustworthiness and ability to accept and tolerate the rejection and pain that he had not the resources to cope with as a child, Paul became less contemptuous and more able to acknowledge his needs (of course, what he was actually doing was splitting off and denying his *own* vulnerability and projecting it into his therapist; so that he was in effect showing how contemptuous he was of his infantile needs).

One of the positive indications in Paul's case was the accessibility and richness of his symbolic material. In the first session he drew a squashed sad looking cat which, like his own cat, was called Moses. His therapist, understanding that this was also a communication about *Paul's* predicament, made a connection between the sad-looking cat and the fact that Moses, like Paul, was also someone who had been given away as a baby and adopted. Feeling understood by his therapist, Paul was able to expand on the theme of being an abandoned child and explore what it meant to him. This showed, that at an unconscious level (all Paul's 'communications' were made through play or drawings – he rarely spoke openly to his therapist), he *wanted* to make contact and to find a way of communicating about issues which were too difficult for him to deal with at a conscious level.

Another positive factor related to the 'feelings' which being with Paul aroused in his therapist. In psychoanalytic work with highly disturbed or pre-verbal children, the way in which the patient is relating both to himself and the therapist is communicated by way of the emotions which are generated within the therapeutic context (see under 'Transference' and 'Countertransference' below). In Paul's case, in spite of the overt expressions of disinterest and contempt, his therapist felt very warmly towards him and saw this as an emotional response to the sad, abandoned, and vulnerable part of Paul.

Whilst we can see from these two cases, that it is by no means always a straightforward matter to assess the resources within a child available to be mobilized in the therapeutic endeavour, there is general agreement concerning the more obvious indications for which one can look. Before one sees the child it is possible to have some idea about the severity of the disturbance and its duration. If the child is clearly communicating his or her distress or is asking for help, then we can assume that he or she is motivated and is 'owning' their distress. Perhaps the most important question to ask is 'To what extent is this child capable of making a relationship?' The therapist also has to assess the way in which the child's defences are organized. Are they brittle, rigid, and inflexible or are they amenable to modification?

As the word implies, defences are there for just that purpose – to defend the personality against external (or internal) threat. However, whilst one should respect defences which the child patient brings with him into therapy, if the thing which they are protecting him against is so unthinkable or unendurable that the child is completely encapsulated and walled off from 'reality', then the chances of reaching through to the child in the first place in order to modify them is greatly reduced.

However, if the child's defences leave a 'door' through which the therapist can communicate, we then have the means of assessing the degree to which the child is open to contact. The key to the 'door' through which access may be gained to the child's unconscious phantasy life can be obtained by way of the therapist's ability to understand and to interpret the symbolic or metaphoric content of the child's communications – whether in words, play, drawings, body posture, or other non-verbal means of expression.

In addition to the above, we would need to take into account the ego strength of the child, his or her natural vitality and determination to resist and fight against whatever is causing distress. Finally, one would want to know how committed the parents or primary care-workers are in ensuring that the child's therapy is supported and protected from disruption for as long as it needs to continue.

THE PSYCHOANALYTIC RELATIONSHIP

We now need to look at what actually 'happens' – or is supposed to happen – once the child is taken on in therapy. In order to do this, we need to have a look at some of the essential elements that constitute the psychoanalytic relationship. Physically, and in terms of external reality, it is defined and circumscribed by always occurring in the same place and at the same time. At the outset, this provides some degree of predictability and consistency for the child. This is important. Many child patients have never had the experience of a safe, constant, predictable relationship with an adult who has a 'space'[13] in his or her mind for them. The failure to provide such a 'containing' space – both physical and mental – can very quickly lead to the breakdown of therapy.

The transference

Another important ingredient is the unique character of the relationship itself. The mere fact of two people coming together at regular intervals in a shared space brings into play some very powerful forces. The intense nature of the feelings, thoughts, or impulses which can be liberated in analytic work go under the heading of 'Transference Phenomena'. These relate to any attitudes, thoughts, or feelings attributed by the patient on to the person of the therapist which are *not commensurate* with the *actual* situation. These are understood by the therapist as repetitive patterns of interpersonal behaviour which were established in early childhood and which are now being displaced on to the therapist. The emotions which become activated as a result of the transference may be either positively or negatively charged.

The positive transference

Positive feelings towards the therapist, such as warmth, affection, admiration, even love, can be important in the early stages of therapy in motivating the patient to continue in therapy. They facilitate the important process of 'engaging' or joining with the therapist, which is necessary for analytic work to begin. However, as pointed out above in relation to Paul, it is not always the case that patients *consciously* join with the therapist in a 'therapeutic alliance'. As with Paul, their conscious attitude may be one of contempt or indifference. In these cases, it can require quite a high degree of skill and tolerance on the part of the therapist in order to both recognize the positive signs by way of which the child is communicating his or her need for help, without retaliating (by rejecting the child) or giving up in despair (the hopelessness which many therapists feel in relation to children who cannot 'own' their need for help is in any case often a 'countertransference response' in which the therapist is literally experiencing *for the child* what the child cannot experience for him- or herself).

The negative transference

This leads us on to an examination of the negative responses such as: hate, anger, envy, fear, which may be directed on to the person of the therapist. In their own way, and provided they are handled properly, these are of no less value than the positive feelings of the child. This is because many of the children who are taken on in therapy have never experienced a relationship with an adult in which it is safe or acceptable to reveal the full extent of their aggression, sadness, desolation, and despair. This may be because they have felt that they needed to 'protect' a parent whom they considered vulnerable in some way, or because of fear of retaliation. The ambivalent feelings which children can have towards such unacceptable emotions can be seen from the following example.

> David, a 4 year-old boy, had just returned to therapy after double operations on his club feet. He showed his anger towards me, and his jealousy of my other patients – for him experienced as my 'other' babies – in the following piece of

play. He had brought some toys with him (two little girl figures and a baby figure) and began the session by making an attack on them. He wanted me to 'blindfold them' so that they could not see and then wanted me to 'make a fire and put them on it'. When I commented that he seemed to want to burn the babies he thought I had been seeing when he was in hospital, he replied, 'Yes, burn the babies.' However, his burning attacks on my other 'analytical' babies soon became reintrojected[14] to show how devastated he felt inside. He had piled more and more dolls on to the fire until it was toppling and then he said, 'This is funny isn't it? All dead. Put baby in ambulance. Baby dead. I'm dead.'[15]

However, whilst this little boy often perceived me as an uncaring parent whom he had to punish or even attack, he was able to retain at some level the notion of me as also being a supportive and protective figure. This underlying positive connection (by counter-acting his more destructive feelings) enabled him to express negative emotions without being overwhelmed with anxiety about having damaged me or the relationship beyond repair (he was originally placed with foster parents because his mother could not cope with his aggressive and destructive behaviour).

The particular value to the child of experiencing a therapeutic relationship in which his or her more destructive feelings and impulses are accepted, tolerated, and understood lies in the oppor-tunity it offers the child to restructure or modify entrenched patterns of relating to itself or others which have become outmoded, mala-daptive, and no longer functional. It provides the child with an opportunity – over a structured period of time – repeatedly to 'work through' or re-enact old patterns of behaviour but with a *different* resolution or outcome.

THERAPEUTIC SKILLS

Because the patterns of behaviour of emotionally disturbed children are frequently intensely disturbing, analytic psychotherapy requires – even demands – a high degree of expertise from the therapist. Perhaps first and foremost, he or she has to know how to 'notice what they are noticing'[16] and be able to unravel any potentially meaningful communications in what they are observing. Once the transference relationship has been established, this means observing not just the child's behaviour but also *one's own responses* to it (technically, this is called 'working in the countertransference'). This requires that the therapist is able to discriminate between 'feelings which belong to the child' and which are being projected into him, and his or her own feelings.

Containment and holding

Psychoanalysts have long known the importance of the therapist's ability to be able to 'hold', or to act as a container for, experiences which the patient cannot consciously 'own' or acknowledge. As a process, it is not so dissimilar to what a mother does for her baby when she 'takes on board' the baby's distress. In so doing, she acts in the first instance as a 'dustbin' or 'nappy' into which the baby can dump or evacuate experiences which it cannot process or integrate. However, she does more than this. She also metabolizes or detoxifies those overwhelming emotions and sensations which are beyond the baby's capacity to digest or assimilate. In a similar manner, the therapist uses his or her emotional responses to the patient as a means of understanding what the latter cannot express solely with words. Ideally, the therapist can then process or think about the child's communications and, by interpreting them, make them more accessible to be dealt with at a conscious level.

Interpretation – the agent of change

Interpretation is the *sine qua non* of analytic psychotherapy. It is the means by which the unknown can become known, resistances and defences overcome, and the agent by way of which real change can occur. As such, it is a very powerful therapeutic tool which requires a precise understanding of what it can and cannot do, and when it can and cannot be used.

First and foremost, an interpretation should be a considered response to something the child is telling the therapist he or she wants help with now. It should never be used as a means for the therapist to use therapeutic insight in order to give the child information which he or she is not yet ready to receive. To do so would leave the child-patient feeling persecuted and intruded upon by the therapist. This means that the 'timing' of interpretations is an important factor in deciding how they will be received by the patient and in his or her capacity to make use of them.

But what exactly is an 'interpretation' in the psychoanalytic sense of the word? It is not merely commenting on what a patient is saying or doing and neither is it giving him or her 'information'. It *is* a way of giving structure, meaning, and purpose to sometimes apparently meaningless and unconnected utterances. As such, it is a technique or model for thinking about language (and non-verbal behaviour) at a meta level. In making interpretations, the therapist is generating hypotheses based on his or her understanding of the *symbolic* content of the child's communications. This means that in order to formulate an interpretation the therapist has to *restructure his or her thinking* from operating solely on a linear, logical, deductive mode, to one which can operate on *two levels* at the same time: one which can cope with analysing meaning at a literal causal level, while at the same time addressing meaning at a metaphorical level. The following examples should illustrate how an interpretation is both a clinical technique for interacting with the patient's unconscious as well as a way of thinking symbolically.

Early on in his therapy with me an adolescent boy produced the following dream:

> On the way to his session with me he saw a large brass telescope in the window of an antique shop. It could magnify 10 times and he thought it was really good but unfortunately it was attached to an ornate chair and he did not think he would be able to use it outside to see the stars. He could not make up his mind between the telescope, which cost £37.00 and membership of his father's golf club which was £25.00. He thought that if it was not attached to the chair it would be cheaper as the chair probably put the price up. The woman in the shop said it was a valuable instrument and well worth the price he would have to pay. He then noticed that the telescope had gold bits on it.

> The only association he had to the dream was seeing a telescope in one of the windows of the clinic where I saw him. It seems here that the telescope is linked with my ability to observe and to focus on distant events. The fact that it was prominently displayed in the antique shop and made of precious metal suggested that it was both a valuable asset as well as being an instrument with which one could look into the past in

order to see things in close-up. It was also an admission from my patient that he needed help in seeing things in this way and could not do it without the telescope. The ornate chair seemed to be linked to my chair and to his desire for *my* telescope – that is, my ability to see inside him – but without having to be tied to me. Wanting to take it outside represented his urge to 'steal' my 'instrument' as well as his envy of it. The price for the telescope probably related to how much value he placed on me and my abilities as a 'valuable instrument' as opposed to joining the golf club which was a denial of his status as a patient and which gave him membership of 'my' club and equal status with me.

In the above example, one can see how the *same* quality – analytical insight – is both admired and envied, wanted and feared, and how important it is in interpreting this kind of symbolic material to pay attention to these different levels of meaning. There was also another level of meaning to this dream which related to this boy's anxiety about my potency. The wish to possess for himself the valuable telescope also stood for his desire to be more potent than me, but also stirred up his anxiety about my using it (as a symbolic penis) to get inside him.

The second example concerns an 8-year-old girl who had been in therapy with me at the time of my daughter's birth, as a result of which she had to miss two of her therapy sessions. The anniversary of my daughter's first birthday coincided with Easter and my patient wanted to make an Easter card for me to give to her.[17] She seemed to have great difficulty in getting the card the way she wanted it, but at the third attempt she got it right and handed it to me. In the middle of the card she had painted an Easter egg above which she had writtten 'Happy Eatser'. I made a connection between eggs and babies and chocolate and pooh and said that although she *thought* she wanted to give my daughter a present, her true feelings towards her were revealed by her misspelling Easter on her third attempt to turn it into a word which had a very different meaning – Eats(h)er. What she was really showing me was how angry she was with my daughter and how she wanted not to feed her but to poison her, to fill her up with pooh and to turn her into a 'shit' baby. On hearing this interpretation, my patient gave vent to a prolonged burst of laughter saying: 'Yes, she is a shit baby! It was meant!'

Here we can see that the act of interpreting the underlying symbolic content of this material made it possible for this girl to own her destructive and aggressive feelings which otherwise might have been experienced as unacceptable. If her disguised attack on me had not been interpreted, she may have experienced some relief but at the same time would have been anxious at my inability to protect her positive feelings for me from her envious attacks. The interpretation, then, had both a cathartic effect of releasing hidden aggression but had also reassured her that her aggressive phantasies could be contained and thought about.

CURE AND TERMINATION

In considering the question of whether a particular treatment has been successful or not and when it can be brought to an end, it is important to differentiate between those therapeutic approaches which concentrate on symptom relief, and psychoanalytic psychotherapy which does not. This does not mean that analytical psychotherapy should not result in symptom relief but that this is not its *primary* aim. As mentioned above, the aim of analytic psychotherapy is to provide the child with the opportunity – within the transference relationship – to re-experience in the 'here and now' persistent patterns of relating, thinking, or feeling which have become dysfunctional, so that they can become available and amenable to change.

Because psychotherapeutic change occurs within a relationship, it is *the changing nature of the relationship itself* which informs the therapist about changes which are taking place and which provides him or her with the data from which can be assessed any improvement in the child's level of anxiety or in his or her ability to adjust to the demands of reality.

From the perspective of viewing analysis as a developmental process which is facilitated by, as well as expressed through, the transference relationship, it is probably inappropriate to talk about cure – or even termination. Analysis is as much an *attitude* one develops towards oneself, a model for thinking symbolically about one's behaviour and that of others, as it is a technique for relieving distress. There is no 'goal' as such, no disease to be cured or organism to be 'got rid of' – only the ever-unfolding process of understanding why we do what we do, and why it affects us in the way it does.

Initially, of course – and more especially with children – the analyst him- or herself acts as a 'transitional ego' for the patient. Gradually, with increasing insight, lessening anxiety, and accrued trust in the analytic relationship, the child becomes more able *him- or herself* to mediate between conscious and unconscious, between id and ego, and between him- or herself and the current demands of external reality. The child's defences become less rigid and brittle, he or she becomes more open, trusting and tolerant and more self-accepting.

When the child can maintain these qualities *outside* the therapeutic relationship, and is no longer so dependent on the therapist, one can begin the gradual process of weaning him or her away from the therapist and into a more mature and reality-based relationship with the outside world.

NOTES

1 In cases where children are seen privately, it is the concern, commitment, and support of the parents which replaces the support provided by the various child-care workers.

2 From this point onwards, the terms therapy or psychotherapy (unless otherwise stated) will refer to therapy which is based on psychoanalytic principles – for example, working in the Transference, maintaining a non-directive stance, making interpretations, and so on.

3 While this is the ideal, in some contexts in which children receive therapy – for example, hospital wards, school buildings, and so on – these requirements may be impossible to meet.

4 Although foster children are exposed to 'parenting', the short-term nature and uncertainty surrounding it frequently detract from the benefit of being in a family atmosphere.

5 M. Boston and R. Szur (Ed.), *Psychotherapy with Severely Disturbed Children*, London: Routledge & Kegan Paul, 1983.

6 Acknowledging such intense and possibly destructive emotions with respect to one's own parents, as the perpetrators of the abuse, is often experienced as more unacceptable than the original abuse itself.

7 D. W. Winnicott, *The Maturational Processes and the Facilitating Environment*, London: The Hogarth Press, 1976, pp. 145–6.

8 F. M. J. Dale and G. Fredman, 'Transgenerational re-enactment', unpublished manuscript, 1987.

9 This relates to the joining of the patient in a therapeutic alliance.

10 Another example of transgenerational re-enactment.

11 Not used here in the strictly psychoanalytical sense.

12 Both Bion and Winnicott employ similar terminology to describe the process whereby the parent or therapist processes unthinkable or uncontainable emotions on behalf of the patient.
W. R. Bion, 'Attention and interpretation', in *Seven Servants – Four Works by W. R. Bion*, New York: Jason Aronson, 1977, p. 106ff.
Winnicott, op. cit., pp. 43–6.
13 This refers to an internal attitude of the therapist which is accepting and tolerant towards the patient.
14 Taken back inside.
15 F. M. J. Dale, 'The body as bondage: work with two children with physical handicap', *Journal of Child Psychotherapy* 9(1) (1983).
16 F. M. J. Dale, 'Baby observation: some reflections on its value and application in the clinical setting', Paper presented at Esther Bick Commemoration Day, May 1984.
17 It is accepted practice in psychoanalytic psychotherapy *not* to reveal details of one's private life. However, this patient gained the information from another source.

Chapter Seven

RESISTANCE AND CO-OPERATION: THE NEED FOR BOTH

A further study of psychotherapy in a Day Unit[1]

DILYS DAWS

I work in a psychiatric Day Unit attached to a Child Guidance Clinic, officially a hospital school. I have described elsewhere[2] the particular issues involved in working in individual psychotherapy with children in the place where the child spends his or her school-days. In this chapter my interest is in looking at how psychotherapy fits into the institution. I give a clinical example of a case where I felt I could attempt psychotherapy with a disturbed little girl with the backing and support of the Day Unit. Although I give much specific detail of how the professions relate in one particular institution, I hope that anyone involved in the setting up of therapy for children will be reminded of their own relevant network, be it families, general practitioners, or teachers at ordinary schools.

The Day Unit differs essentially from, for example, a school for maladjusted children in that it is a National Health Service facility with a consultant psychiatrist as head of the Unit. There is a part-time psychiatric staff of four, the psychiatrist, a social worker, educational psychologist, and child psychotherapist. However, the Unit is run as a school by a teacher-in-charge who is one of three full-time Inner London Education Authority teachers with one part-time Inner London Education Authority remedial teacher, and three full-time nursery assistants employed by the National Health Service. The other staff are a full-time secretary/administrator, a caretaker, and a cook, all National Health Service employees.

The Unit was founded some 15 years ago by staff of the parent clinic, and seen then, among its other uses, as a Unit where children in therapy could be placed. Over the years it has been seen by referrers in the community, psychiatrists in other Child Guidance

Clinics, teachers, educational psychologists, Educational Welfare Officers, and so on as a place to refer children who for many disparate reasons have broken down in their normal schools. These are children who may or may not benefit from psychotherapy. The Unit offers a relatively short-term placement averaging 2 years, and during these years it is hoped that the child will be able to recover from the personal breakdown or disintegration that often accompanies the breakdown of their school placement. That is, as with clinic referrals, a child and his or her family may have to concentrate on and exaggerate their difficulties in order to precipitate the help that is needed.

When a child is placed on the Day Unit, there is often an enormous feeling of relief that the difficulties of managing in a large school are no longer there. Although, of course, this may be something of a 'honeymoon' experience, the relief of not having to deal with a large complicated institution remains, and children can begin to sort out their problems in a small supportive unit.

The average 2 year stay allows time for a child to recover from this first stage of breakdown, and for a therapeutic reintegrative process to occur before the child is referred on to a long-term placement; either back into the normal school system or into special education of some kind, day or residential, or into residential hospital placement. The range of problems dealt with at the Day Unit is very wide, and providing a suitable therapeutic experience for all these children adds to the variety and interest of working there. It adds also to the tensions and conflicts for staff in trying to decide what is best for children with such different needs.

The Day Unit is divided into three small groups, roughly according to age, each taken by a teacher and assistant. The idea of having two members of staff to each group is intrinsic to the Unit. Each pair provides a model of a parental couple, irrespective of their particular sex, a model of a couple working together, using individual differences and characteristics in partnership for the benefit of the child. As well as acting as a model the couple are a support for each other: when absorbing the projections of a very disturbed child it is essential to be able to catch the eye of a partner who is not being overwhelmed by these projections. The teacher who is with the child can then perhaps manage to stay emotionally with him or her and contain the projections without being tempted to fling them back at the child.

This brings us to a definition of what constitutes 'therapy' in a therapeutic setting. The Day Unit is thought of as a therapeutic unit. The three groups are run as classroom groups and the children have school lessons and other school-based activities and outings for much of the day. Some but not all of the children have individual remedial teaching and some have individual psychotherapy. How is it decided who will have this, and how does it fit in with the work of the Unit as a whole? Like the partnership of teacher and assistant in each group, is there a partnership between the group's teacher-couple and the individual therapist that some children have?

The ambience of the Day Unit is psychoanalytically informed: at its simplest this means that all the staff have a knowledge that the unconscious exists; that disturbed children are in the grip of unresolved unconscious conflicts; and that the way to help them lies in providing a contained understanding structure where they can express these conflicts and work through them.

This working through can be at two levels, one where the conflict remains unconscious but is responded to appropriately; and second, where connections are made for the child so that the unconscious becomes to differing degrees conscious. Our everyday problem concerns how much of each of these processes is relevant for any particular child, which is more therapeutically effective, and who should do it? Is interpretation the province only of the psychotherapist or should the teacher on the spot say the obvious and give the sort of psychic first aid that some children seem to call out for? If a teacher does make an interpretation, can the child actually bear it in the classroom without privacy, or alternatively will it feel as though permission has been given to use the classroom as an individual psychotherapy setting?

Let us go back to the reasons for referral to the Day Unit. These seem to come at two different levels of conceptualizing a problem. One kind of referral comes from Child Guidance Clinics where a psychiatric assessment has already been made that the child is in need of individual psychotherapy, and may already be in therapy at that clinic; the other broad category is simply that the child is no longer able to maintain daily attendance at a local normal or special school, and is felt to be in need of the special attention that a small unit can offer.

In all these cases a rigorous diagnostic procedure is offered to each child by the Day Unit. The child and family are seen by the psychiatrist, educational psychologist, and social worker, and by the teacher-in-charge and the teacher in the group into which the child might be taken. This diagnostic procedure serves to assess the suitability or otherwise of the child for the Day Unit, and vice versa. It can also serve as a consultation by an experienced team in formulating the nature of an elusive problem and suggesting other more suitable facilities. Offering of a place to a child depends on the feeling that he or she will personally make use of the Unit, and also on the balance of the appropriate age-groups at any one moment. It seems to work best to have a variety of personalities and problems in each group, so that any one does not consist entirely of, say, withdrawn non-speaking children, or conversely of acting-out impulsive ones.

This diagnostic and selection procedure determines who is felt to be suitable for the Day Unit; that is, who could make good use of its therapeutic environment as a whole. How, then, does psychotherapy fit in?

Paradoxically for a therapeutic unit committed to working psychodynamically it does not always augur well for psychotherapy already to have been recommended at the time of referral to the Unit. When a child is already in psychotherapy or when there is a strong expectation that psychotherapy will be set up when the child starts at the Unit, a feeling of resistance to the therapy may build up in the Day Unit. Where does this feeling stem from and what does it mean? It is easy to dismiss such feelings as resistance to psychoanalytic thinking, to a difficulty in sharing a child with the therapist, to envy of the specific skill of the therapist, or of the confidential intimate relationship between child and therapist. Of course, some elements of all this may exist, in fact perhaps they should exist. If psychotherapy is the rigorous, disturbing, absorbing experience we claim it to be for therapist and patient alike, can we expect the colleagues close at hand to this process to confine themselves to an absent-mindedly benevolent support? Strong feelings will be aroused, not all of them friendly, and this is part of our shared working situation.

I think we should take this as seriously as Freud found he had to take the resistance of his patients to psychoanalysis. We should take it that resistance is not an awkward phenomenon that can be ignored, reasoned away, or removed by high-powered trickery.

Resistance in a patient is a resistance to change in the personality. It shows us that the pain involved in making a change is felt at the time to be even greater than the pain involved in keeping inadequate functioning going. The psychoanalyst or therapist who can help a patient successfully negotiate this change is the one who can remain with it and see the struggle itself as the instrument of change. The resistance that some members of a multiprofessional working unit sometimes show towards psychotherapy must equally be taken seriously as an intrinsic aspect of the dynamic working of the Unit, and we must learn from it.

It must not become polarized so that some individuals feel themselves pushed into the position of being anti-therapy and others to have an unrealistically optimistic expectation of it. It is more helpful to acknowledge the ambivalence about therapy that is within us all, even therapists (or even especially therapists). Therapeutic zeal is more credible when tempered with a little depressive doubt. Alternatively we cannot allow this resistance to block the setting up of psychotherapy – to act as a veto. It is only valuable as a dimension of the struggle towards change.

Psychotherapy in a therapeutic environment represents an essence, a distillation of the work going on every day within this environment. The sessions of individual psychotherapy may be an enhanced experience inside the therapy room of what goes on outside it – the child brings the same sort of play material to the therapy, makes the same sort of confidences about him- or herself to the therapist as to his teacher. The difference is that with the teacher the child gets a broad acceptance and understanding of him- or herself and personal conflicts; with the therapist the child may get a specific and detailed verbal interpretation which helps him or her to make a link between conscious and unconscious personal knowledge. Both teacher and therapist may be efficiently helping the child to move on to another level of self-knowledge and ability to use his or her intellectual and emotional facilities more effectively.

In other children the use of classroom and therapy is apparently more separate. The child may focus bringing his or her unconscious conflicts into the therapy sessions and be free to use the classroom more straightforwardly and concentrate on learning. One patient of mine, a little boy of 6, was observed by his teachers to shake himself each time he came back into the classroom after his therapy session. He seemed to need to shake off the internal preoccupations of his therapy in order to re-enter the everyday external world.

A child like this shows how painful the transition can be from inner to outer reality. We all know the children who cannot let themselves make this difficult transition and keep the boundaries intact; they noisily come to and from their therapy, they disturb the classroom before, and particularly after, their sessions. By not knowing when to start and when to stop their session they never fully experience being alone with the therapist in the seclusion of the therapy room. They break the confidentiality of their own therapy as though the drama around it mattered more to them than the therapy itself. The pain for this sort of child in moving in and out of his therapy is often projected into the adults around and becomes dramatized by them. When teachers and therapist feel themselves to be in conflict with each other about therapy it is worth examining it in terms of conflicting feelings the child cannot hold inside himself.

Winnicott said something like, 'There is no such thing as a baby. Only a baby and its mother.' Similarly, perhaps there is no such thing as a child in therapy – only a child, its parents, and the therapist. In a Unit such as ours the support to a child in therapy may often be not the actual parents, but a parenting aspect of the teachers and other staff. Children cannot go off to therapy from a vacuum – even if they journey themselves, they need to be sent and received back by someone. If they are not, then the therapist may find him- or herself inappropriately trying to fulfil aspects of a parental role, instead of being free to receive transference of feelings about parental figures. A patient of mine, an 11-year-old girl in care, was living in a children's home that was rapidly disintegrating and shortly afterwards closed. I was able to support a plan which enabled her eventually to be fostered. In the meantime, as I drove home after seeing her I had unfinished thoughts on the lines of 'Fostering is more use to children in care than psychotherapy.' My point is that it was not only this girl's parentlessness which gave rise to a sentimental fantasy from both her and myself that if only I would foster her all would be well. It was her lack of *substitute* parents, of someone to take immediate care of her and responsibility for her in a real way outside of the therapy, that was so painfully obvious to us both.

In the Day Unit it is often the teaching staff who provide support for the child in therapy. This can in some cases be the only support the child gets for his or her therapy. It sometimes seems worthwhile within the Unit to attempt therapy with children from disturbed families who would find it very difficult to support therapy at a clinic either emotionally or practically. It then becomes the Unit staff who offer the emotional containment and the assumption of an everyday knowledge of the child's state of emotional development. They do this instead of the parents. In other cases the staff simply stand in for parents because they are present at the school and the parents are not. They send the child to sessions and they receive the child back, but it is as an extension of the parents care for their child, not as a substitute for it.

If teaching staff in such a situation have a parental role to fill in the support of therapy, have they not also some parental rights? This is an excessive way of stating it, perhaps, but I think it is unrealistic to expect enthusiastic support for therapy unless the staff members concerned have had some involvement in the process of deciding a child could benefit from therapy. It has been said that children have therapy because someone wants them changed. It may well be that children are referred because they are a nuisance to someone; even the referral of a quiet depressed child may be because it upsets someone to see the child like that. What matters for us in this concept is that if someone wants a child changed then they know that child as he or she is – the dissatisfaction with the child has a positive function and includes a relationship between referrer and child – something within the referrer connects with the child and feels all is not well. If this process has already happened and the child is already in therapy, staff may never feel so engaged with the therapy, and may resent or question the need for it.

This process also holds in selection for the Unit. Teaching staff have told me how the method of admission to the Unit of one little boy, Mario, from a powerful but tragic family from abroad, had coloured their feeling about him in the classroom. This 6-year-old boy, an obvious victim of circumstances, has a tiresomely imperious manner. His teachers have coped with much more difficult behaviour from the disturbed children they teach. It was they, not me, who made a link between their lack of sympathy with Mario's imperiousness and the high-handed way in which enthusiastic therapists and psychiatrists had eased his route from a teaching hospital to the Unit and analysis five times a week. Delicate negotiations had gone on with his capricious parents. Consultation within the Unit had been virtually nil. The normal admission procedure, which allows two opportunities for the staff to consider a new entry, had been curtailed and the teachers in the group never had the opportunity to make a place inside themselves for Mario.

We all know the disruption that premature births can cause to parents who had not quite got themselves ready; we know how the outcome of an adoption can be influenced by the way in which the introduction is handled and by how much preparation time the adoptive parents have had before they receive the baby. It is not far-fetched to suggest that professionals offering a child special care in a special unit need a recognized way of making room inside themselves for each new disturbed child who comes into the Unit. Leading on from this I suggest that when a child enters therapy, a prerequisite is that the teachers who are intimately involved with him or her need to discover afresh for that child from within themselves the need for therapy.

The reality is not as piously co-operative as this might sound. A teacher may say, 'John is threatening the other children with the scissors. I think he needs therapy', and the therapist reply, 'I don't feel like seeing him if he is like that.' The serious issue behind this interchange is, 'Who is responsible for this child's aggression – can it be pushed on to the therapist or can classroom and therapy share the experience of it?' Similarly, can we share a child's depression?; and, more seriously, the experience of a psychotic child? These last are the most tragic to deal with and the therapy of psychotic children remains a dilemma within our Unit. We have had several experiences where the pain of these children has become nakedly revealed. They have become apparently much more disturbed and the disturbance resounds through the Unit psychically as well as physically. Deeply felt and sincere differences of opinion among the professional staff about the validity of such therapy make us all question our theoretical and instinctive position each time.

To redress the balance, in many of our cases psychotherapy is set up after we have all observed that a child is already benefiting from the general therapeutic setting of the Unit. In these cases our expectation of what psychotherapy can achieve will be coloured by the therapeutic alliance the child has engaged in with the staff he or she already knows. The therapist thus builds on the goodwill other staff have created. One might expect goodwill to surround the therapy. Even so, through the most apparently tranquil therapy we would do well not to forget the reverberations that run through each of us connected with the child. Therapy is going to stir up feelings, in the child, in the therapist, and in colleagues. A therapeutic unit is supposed to be able to stand such feelings. If we look at the setting for therapy with too much delicacy we can find ourselves condoning our own laziness or moral cowardice.

In our Unit I am the permanent psychotherapist and see two or three children at any one time. The psychiatrist also sees children and we have a trainee psychotherapist and a registrar who have training cases at the Unit. Some children may already be in therapy at an outside clinic, or our own clinic. Others are seen by therapists coming up to the Day Unit. We have increasingly found that in spite of the difficulties of organization in having several therapists working in the Unit, this outweighs the disadvantages of having the therapy at a distance, even the short one to our own clinic. It seems as though the more a therapist can be a part of the Day Unit, the more they can have face-to-face contact with the staff working full time in the Unit, the more the child's therapy is protected. Visiting therapists vary in style from those who can spare the time to have lunch or coffee at the Unit, or who *know* when the teacher has a break in order to phone him or her then; to those who apparently see themselves as autonomous and, for example, arrange holidays without enquiring as to how this relates to Day Unit breaks.

I hold occasional seminars, some with the therapists only, some with therapists and teachers together, where we hope to discuss the issues, to say to each other some of the things there is never time or occasion for in daily work. We often start with the specific technical problem of how a therapist takes a child from classroom to therapy room. The minutiae of detail of whether the therapist goes into the classroom, whether the teacher sends the child out over the threshold, and the many idiosyncratic variations that difficult children drive us to devise – these seem to me to sum up in a nutshell the basic problem: how does a child negotiate his way from teacher to therapist and how do we help him to do so? It is a wise therapist who does not attempt to start a child's session at a time when he or she is playing in the garden. If the child is showing even a modicum of reluctance to come to therapy, the wide open spaces literally put the child beyond anyone's reach. He or she is too far away to feel the containment from either side, and no one's job description includes running round the garden to fetch children for therapy. I mention this, obvious though it sounds, because I think the way we show mutual good faith is in the first place setting up practical arrangements that work. Times must be arranged that are mutually convenient, that acknowledge the importance of the school timetable and of the therapist's timetable, and of the experience for children of when they come out of the school routine and when they go back into it.

This is our first provision. If we can do this within the very real limitations, then one enormous source of mutual irritation is gone. If the timing is badly wrong for the classroom then every time the therapist knocks and puts his or her head round the classroom door, the teacher will *not* feel that the therapy is an extension of his or her work with the child; the teacher will feel it breaks into and diminishes the value of his or her work. A therapist fitting uncomfortably into the school timetable, and rushing up the hill from another patient, may not have the space and readiness to take in a child's disturbance. The therapist will feel persecuted by both patient and institution.

If we get this very basic framework right and if therapists and teachers feel comfortable with each other, then both are in a better position to take on the child's projections. It often happens that once a child is in therapy, the severe states of being are much increased. The temptation is of course to attribute the pain of this to someone else. Therapists, teachers, and parents all feel that someone else is stirring up, or failing to contain, aggression, depression, or whatever else is in question. Therapists are the most likely culprits and patients share this view. One articulate boy of 9 assured me, 'You make my life a misery.' It is sometimes hard to hold on to the knowledge that it was someone's misery that *brought* them to therapy, and that competent therapy provides an opportunity to transfer on to the therapist the miseries and conflicts of his previous relationships and experience. This we find can take place most effectively in a separate, private, and confidential setting.

Here we have a dilemma. So far in this chapter I have described how I think that getting together to provide a protective network for a child's therapy is an important prerequisite. I have suggested that if therapist and teacher know each other face to face they are less likely to misinterpret the other's dealings with the child. The dilemma is this – if we take this too far and therapist and teacher understand each other too well – if they have too many dealings with each other, then there will be no space for the child's therapy. I repeat that therapy is essentially a private and confidential business, sometimes a lonely business. If all is shared then perhaps there will be nothing to share. Both therapist and teacher have to use their mutual goodwill to tolerate the point at which they can no longer work together. They have to tolerate for themselves a point of separation and they have to help the child cross the bridge from one to another and back again.

This does not mean each one abrogating his or her own area of authority. My colleague, Jo Jacobs, has pointed out to me that difficulty in defining boundaries can lead to diffidence on both sides. Neither wants to obtrude into the other's territory, and the child is left wondering to whom he or she belongs. Because our colleagues in the classroom are themselves concerned to protect the confidentiality of the therapy, they may withdraw from action when the therapist appears. At one level I am talking about the occasional child who needs a firm physical handing over from teacher to therapist. More generally there is implied a psychic handover, i.e. an implicit understanding from teacher to child that he or she knows what sort of thing he or she is sending the child off to, and what sort of experience the child has had on coming back. Many of the children in our Unit cannot stand separations. The material of their therapy may be pervaded with them and the comings and goings from therapy symbolize separation for them every time. If teacher and therapist can make an empathic leap with the child into the other's territory each way, then the child is helped to manage the dangers.

I said earlier that when we find ourselves in conflict about a child's therapy, the key is in the conflicting feelings within the child. It often appears that conflicts are expressed not by rows but by failures of communication. We are all guilty of these. What do they mean? The failures occur first in one professional failing to pass on some arrangement made in the course of their own work with the child, which affects other colleagues. More seriously, one part of the team finds itself making plans that affect the child's future without discussing these with other members of the team. We all do it. What possesses us? It seems to me that at these times we are overtaken by the projection of the child's anxieties, or someone else's anxiety about the child. If these anxieties only take account of one aspect of the child's needs, that is one aspect of conflicting feelings, then the worker may be swayed by the strength of this and act accordingly.

This sort of situation occurs at times in decisions about a child leaving the Unit. Often it is impossible for us to have a consensus of opinion about the right time for a child to leave. The time-scale for therapy is often much longer than the useful time that a child can stay in the Unit. A feeling of movement in the child's life urges on a change of school, only the therapist wants more time to resolve infantile conflicts. One side feels that the other is blinkered to the child's real interests. For many children therapy is only possible within the framework of the Unit. When the natural momentum of the Unit's work comes to an end, or when with more disturbed children the Unit and often the home can no longer satisfactorily contain them, then it seems obvious on one level that the child should be placed elsewhere. It is ironical that the aspect of the Unit that is a holding for therapy can disappear at a moment when the therapist feels that the child most needs a promise of continuity. Differing views of the child's needs seem irreconcilable, and the decisions we make seem arbitrary. Perhaps again we pick up the child's own panic about separation – difficulties in negotiating the way in which a child leaves the Unit may represent the enormous conflict within the child and his or her readiness to leave. Between us we hold the range of the child's feelings – even if he or she cannot, can we dare to put them together?

One child I had in therapy provides examples of many of the problems I have outlined. The problems of separation, and the concept of privacy also prevailed. This is not a particularly successful case, but one of interest to me and members of staff, and contains many examples of how we have co-operated or not in the course of her therapy.

JOSEPHINE

I started to see Josephine once weekly after she had been in our Day Unit for a year. She was an obviously disturbed, unhappy little girl of 6, with a serious eye defect following a car crash when she was aged 2. Josephine was the fifth child in the family and had a brother a year younger than herself. This family was chaotic and there was much obvious stress. The older children had various artistic talents and were successful academically. Josephine had been excluded from her primary school for her unruly behaviour before coming to the Day Unit and her self-esteem was low.

Josephine's therapy was set up by mutual agreement in the Unit. There was a feeling that she was responding well to the therapeutic environment of the Unit and was ready to take therapy 'on board'. I met her parents with the social worker of the Unit, and found them in despair about their daughter. It seemed to me that they were so occupied with the problems of the family in general, and the severity of Josephine's disturbance, that the offer of therapy made little impact on them. In fact I subsequently had very few dealings with her parents. They never initiated contact themselves, although they were always friendly when I spoke to them on the phone and agreed readily when I offered a second weekly session, a few weeks after we started. I was a bit taken aback when I went up to them at a parents' evening and they failed to recognize me.

So with Josephine it was very much her own teachers, and the Day Unit staff in general, with whom I discussed the progress of her treatment and her state of development. When, for example, I offered a second session it was at the suggestion of her class teacher, who observed that a week was too long for her to wait between sessions.

In the first session her teacher, Mrs D, offered, as she usually does, to accompany Josephine and I to my room. Josephine is the only child who has refused this offer – she made a pushing-away gesture with her hand, and then walked to my room as though she knew the way. This was the first example for me of her constant determination to be in control. In the room she dashed to a desk, opened a drawer, and was disconcerted to find it empty. I pointed out her own drawer of toys, opened ready for her in a chest of drawers at the other side of the room. She tried all the other drawers, found them to be locked, except for the top empty one which has a broken lock. She closed her own and said, 'Where's my drawer? It's locked.' I readily concluded that offering anything to Josephine was not going to be straightforward. I suggested that she look at her toys and she took out some coloured bricks and started matching the colours, saying, 'Does green go with yellow?', and so on. I pointed out that the colours she chose matched her dress and mine, and said she might be wondering how well she and I would go with each other. She then became quite exuberant, built towers and made them crash. I was talking about her worries in coming to see

127

me – a strange person in a strange room, and how hard it was for her not to be in charge. She said, 'I think you are feeling worried about me coming to see you.'

We talked about the therapy being a place for *her* to come and play and talk about her worries and she said, 'It's talking therapy', a phrase which came back to us often in later sessions. She decided to paint and made some shapes – I had to guess whether they were a house or a car. Which ever I chose she then made into the opposite. I said she was putting me into the wrong each time – showing me *her* worry about getting things wrong; about being little and not being in control. I said I thought she felt that if she was not in control it would be dreadful – that everything would go wrong.

In this first session I thus learnt two of Josephine's main defences, her attempts to put all her worries into someone else, and her need to control. As therapy progressed I learnt poignantly of the things that had happened to her in reality when she lost this control. I saw her the next week, but the third week I had 'flu. I now quote some of her third session which thus took place after a two-week gap.

Josephine came quickly – dashed upstairs ahead of me – started to go the wrong way – running ahead and stumbled down small stairs, and I told her not to rush. In the room she ran to the drawers – closed her own drawer – opened the top one which is permanently unlocked, and said, looking at me jokingly, 'Where are my things? You threw them in the rubbish bin.' 'That was naughty of me', I joked in return. She laughed, closed the drawer and opened her own. I said she had worried that I hadn't looked after her things properly when I was away.

She said, 'I screamed every day when you weren't here', demonstrated, and kicked me. I said something and she said, 'I hate you because you were away.' I said she was worried that the screaming and the angry feelings had kept me away, and that I wasn't there then to look after the screaming. She said, 'I thought you were dead.' We talked about this through the session. At times she seemed to be parrotting me, at other times genuinely seeing if, for instance, my heart was still beating.

Later in the session she played with plasticine and let me help her make two balls. She put them together to make a

figure, said something about a tummy, then said, 'It split.' She
had been talking about me being away, and about the holiday
coming, and I said she was worried about my tummy being
split and that it was her fault. She turned on me, kicking,
screaming, and spitting. I talked about her worries about the
time when I was ill – that it was her angry feelings with me
that had made me ill. She meanwhile noticed the other set of
drawers in the room and tugged at them. I said that she felt
I had gone off with another baby in my tummy and she was
angry about that. She went on spitting and screaming, and
saying, 'What's frightened? What's worried?' 'You're frightened,
you're worried', and I said the spitting and screaming was to
spit and scream out the frightened feelings, and that she kept
thinking I was going to spit them back into her. She was also
saying 'Piss off' and 'Fuck off' and asked if I would tell her
Mummy. I said it was all private here and I wouldn't tell her
Mummy or her teacher. She put eyes on the plasticine figure
and then said, 'It's got eyes on its tummy.' I asked what she
was thinking about eyes, and she said nothing. I said that when
I had met her Mummy and Daddy they had told me she had
had operations on her eyes. She said 'I haven't. I'm going to
have one.' I said I thought she was telling me about her
worries about the operation. We talked again of her worries that
I was dead when I had 'flu because of what she had done to
me, and what I might do to her, etc. She poked at my face and
eyes as we talked.

She quietened down and started to do letters in her book. She
told me about the children at home, adding one, an imagined
brother Joseph, then naming herself and then her real brother.
She went to the drawers again and we talked about her sharing
her mother at home and me here, with the other children.

She wanted to take her plasticine figure home. I said she
couldn't and she reminded me that I had let her take her
paper model last week. 'You said "I'm not going to take if off
you".' I said it had been a mistake to let her take it, and she
said 'You made a mistake so you've got to let me take this.' I
said the mistake was in not keeping all the things together and
all the feelings together – letting it spill outside the drawer and
the room. She suddenly gave it back to me, then tried to trap
my fingers in the drawer and rushed out of the room and

recklessly downstairs, but slowed down as she got to the classroom.

As you can see, she used therapy from the beginning, has been aware of the possibilities and the rules: she has known it was a 'talking therapy' and words, actions, and emotions have tumbled out. In that third session the issue of privacy came up and was one of the themes of her therapy. She was apparently hurt when she discovered that I would not answer questions about myself, but it became a sort of ironical game – she would ask me a question and then mockingly say 'It's private', which was not, I hasten to say, a quotation from me. The difficulty then was that if I asked *her* a question about home, her almost invariable answer was 'It's private.' I suspect, however, that this was useful as a formula and that it really was difficult for her to tell me in explicit terms about the dealings she had at home with her family. What she did not fail to communicate was the essence of it all in the transference. In fact when she thought I might actually answer a question about myself she became very anxious.

In the school situation she was very keen for me to preserve *her* privacy, but could misuse her relationship with me cruelly towards other children. One needy little girl whose therapy elsewhere had had to stop often said 'Hullo' to me. Josephine said to her 'Don't say hullo to my therapist. She's a stranger to you.' Another time, as she left the classroom to see me, she said meaningfully '*Therapy*, Jonathan' to a child whose therapist was away. In that third session we were able to see how she spits out and screams out the attacks she feels are going to happen to her. When I had been ill with 'flu it seemed she felt that my illness was due to her attacks on me, and that the damaged me would attack *her*, and also be unable to protect her from attack.

Throughout the therapy Josephine has demonstrated that she feels constantly under attack – she is constantly expecting a 'smack in the face'. From her constantly provoking behaviour it seemed likely that her expectations could easily be put into practice.

We have worked on her eye operation, both in preparation and afterwards. After the first one, which took place during her time at the Day Unit, Josephine was able to spend a whole session acting out to me her experience, remembered and fantasized, of being on the operating table at the mercy of the surgeons, and of being blindfolded and helpless afterwards. In many subsequent sessions she acted out a sadistic game in which she and I sat under a blanket in turns, and occasionally together. When I was under the blanket she attacked me from outside and this seemed to be a way of communicating her experience in the dark in hospital. It again illustrated that Josephine's only defence is to project her fears into someone else. She is then terrified of the threat of it all being flung back at her. I hoped that my understanding of her fears would moderate this process and allow her to take it back in manageable doses.

Josephine's parents are unable to prepare her properly for traumatic events such as the eye operations, but I suspect that her extreme vulnerability precedes these betrayals, and that they confirm rather than cause her feelings that she is always under threat. The nature of her disability – an eye defect – in itself was one of the causes of her vulnerability. Because she was literally unable to see clearly she was unable to sift the dangers of her external world. At times it must have seemed to her to be a jumble of persecution. When successive operations helped her to see more clearly, that in itself made her able to relate to the world with less anxiety.

Another theme was that of the birth of her younger brother, which came up in relation to other children in therapy with me. She probed my protection of her time, her toys, her privacy. She asked trick questions about whether I would allow her brother into the therapy room if she said it was all right and seemed satisfied with my absolute holding to the integrity of her therapy. She asked what would happen if he tried 'to smash his way in' and I talked about her feeling that he had smashed his way into Mummy's tummy and into their family and supplanted her as the baby. After this she talked, more distantly, of her elder sisters, and a hardly expressed but poignant feeling that she would never be the same as they were.

Josephine then moved up into an older age-group at the beginning of the new school year. The next term was more difficult, with her screaming increasing. She often screamed at the beginning of a session, then had a quiet half-hour after getting solace from physical contact with me, or sucking her own thumb, and screaming again at the moment of re-entering the classroom. Talking beforehand about the pain of leaving therapy or of her destructive intent towards the children in the classroom did not alleviate this – the containment had to come from her teachers within the classroom.

The two last sessions before Christmas are of interest. In the first of these she sobbed and kicked her way round the room, knocking over furniture and apparently not listening to what I said. In the next session she came in, quickly arranged two chairs touching and facing each other, and said 'Lock my drawer, it's talking today.' She then took me through the sequence of the previous session, asking me to repeat my interpretations. 'What did you say when I kicked the table over?' We talked quietly and calmly of what I felt was her distress about the coming break, which seemed through her eyes to be endless – a black hole of desperation. It appeared to me that she had no surety that I or the Day Unit would be back for her after Christmas; but also that it was not a simple experience of aloneness, or misery, but an active state of persecution in which she, alone, in the darkness, was going to be attacked. I also think that I, as the therapist, had been so attacked and damaged by her that I could not exist in her mind in my absence to convey her across such a break, and I then became one of her attackers. At that point I was not able to break into this dreadful sequence or convincingly see where it derived from; she conveyed it to me repeatedly without being able to get any relief from it.

At the time I wrote this last paragraph Josephine's behaviour in the Unit as a whole was disruptive, and her spitting and screaming spoilt the classroom for the other children in the group. We had a meeting about her and I wrote this in preparation, conveying my doubts about her ability to use therapy. Following our meeting, the psychiatrist and teacher-in-charge spoke formally to Josephine's parents and to her. This had a most marked effect. She listened solemnly and made enormous efforts to curtail both the screaming and the spitting. I perhaps regretted that my interpretations had not alone been able to do this, but I appreciated the way in which the authority of the Day Unit was successful in setting limits for her. She then became able to differentiate her behaviour in therapy and in the rest of the Unit.

She continued to scream and spit in therapy and I struggled to understand it in terms of her need to spit out and scream out the awful fears inside her. The arbitrary way in which her feelings of persecution could erupt were shown in two examples – when I had a bad cold she said in disgust 'I will have to eat your snot', and

132

when I wore a pair of red boots with a zig-zag design she said 'It's a crocodile. It's going to bite me.' Each time I wore them, the sight of the boots triggered off this response, although through repetition it became a joke. Both these instances show how vulnerable she feels to attack and one can sympathize with her parents in their lack of success in protecting her from the persecution of her operations. I think we can see how unusually vulnerable she is and how much more of a prey she is to such fantasies than are most children who undergo such experiences.

Her screaming and spitting subsided except for the unfortunate habit of screaming as she re-entered the classroom after the session. My interpretations became less sympathetic as I could see how she spoiled the quiet of the classroom. An identical grimace of pain and perhaps anger would pass over her teachers' faces and mine as the ear-splitting sound emerged. In fact they then eased this enormously by being ready for her when she appeared. She was bundled into an armchair and held by one of the staff. The sympathy and containment *they* gave her at this moment in fact connected better with the experience she had had within the therapy room than did my own feeling towards her of betraying the resolution of her destructiveness, which we had each time achieved within the room. I was grateful to her teachers for the way they managed this period. Josephine betrayed the very privacy of her sessions which was so important to her when she spilled over in this way. I felt that her teachers made the empathic leap I described earlier, into knowing what she needed, without displaying undue curiosity, or undue criticism of my management of her.

By the next term Josephine's parents had decided she would be better at boarding school, and had discussed it with her. Josephine told me of this and scrutinized the expression on my face. She said 'Is it a sad face or a happy face?' She wanted to know if I was happy to get rid of her, or sad to see her go. We discussed how she could say goodbye to the Unit and to me without spoiling all the good things we had had together; and about how to remember someone inside you when you were no longer with them.

The next session she produced 2p from her dungaree pocket and said 'That's for the therapy.' I said that she did not need to pay me for it, but I knew she was telling me she was grateful for what we had done together. She said with great meaning 'You said *talk*' and I said I thought she was grateful for my helping her talk about things with words instead of screaming and kicking to show her feelings. She then rather spoilt our mood of self-congratulation by spitting in my face. When I protested she said 'Miss B says I can spit in therapy because that's my problem', a rather unconstructive reference back to the talk she had had with the psychiatrist and teacher-in-charge when she had learnt to differentiate her behaviour inside and outside therapy.

One area of protection of me is worth noting here. Throughout her attacking of me she has always protected my handbag, and I have thought of this as being an extension of myself. Before over-turning furniture she carefully lifts my bag and puts it in a corner. In a recent session she said 'I'll put your bag on that chair.' I said 'Thank you' and she said 'I knew you'd say that.' I have never risked interpreting this split and spoiling the bag's special status but I think her acknowledgement of my thanks has meaning for her.

In recent sessions she had told me obliquely of her masturbation, which I felt was partly connected with her anger in bed at night at feeling excluded by me and by her parents. She continued some overtly sexual display – wanting to take off her knickers and finally in one session asked me to smack her (fully-clothed) bottom. My interpretations did not divert her, and in order to further the work I joined in the game and pretended to smack her. The results were illuminating. She retaliated on me and I said I thought she believed this was what mummies and daddies did in bed together and how they made babies. Then I said I thought she was trying to smack the babies out of mummy's inside. Josephine was delighted with this remark and repeated it many times. The next session she began by chanting 'Smack the baby out' and tried to reinstate the game. I was then inspired to say that I thought Josephine really wanted to be my baby and mummy's baby, and have lots and lots of cuddles. She did not know how to get me to give them to her, and at home she did not know how to get mummy to give them to her, so she tried to get smacked instead and was naughty until mummy smacked her. Josephine said 'How do you know about home?' and I said I didn't, I was working it out from what she told me. She came up close and spat straight in my face and I said I also thought spitting might be kissing – that she really wanted to be close and kiss people but she spat instead because she didn't know if they would want to kiss her. She became very clinging and got me to tuck her up in a blanket on the couch. She was very reluctant to leave and asked if she could marry me. I said how hard it was to leave me and the Day Unit when she went to her new school and she said 'You can't marry ladies.' She got up quietly, got me to carry her down the corridor, and went quietly back to her classroom.

In another session she again asked me to marry her but in a joking 'referring-back' way. Then she said she would like to have babies but not to get married, so she would find a good friend and ask him to make a baby with her. I asked her why she didn't want to get married, and she said she didn't want to sleep in the same bed as someone.

The poignancy is that it is very difficult to envisage this little girl as managing marriage or parenthood. Although we could see her worry about marriage as an Oedipal defence, it seems more likely that her enormous problems about separation are the key. She can only see herself as totally merged or totally separate. The end of a therapy session is so impossible to contemplate that she goes from being my baby in a blanket, wrapped in timeless care, to merging infinitely with me in marriage. What she cannot be is a little girl walking separately down the corridor after her session. I think her repudiation of marriage is like her eliciting of smacks instead of cuddles, her spitting instead of kissing. She cannot stand a closeness that includes endings and separations so she forfeits the closeness.

Meanwhile we are working on an ending; of her time in therapy, at the Day Unit, and at home. We have talked about how to take in and keep things good inside her and she has told me that her teacher suggested taking photographs away with her. She worries that we are sending her off to a school that has the cane, and has asked if the teachers there will be patient. She jokingly tells me that the teacher-in-charge has arranged for me to go with her to boarding school so that she can have therapy there. I find this quite a hopeful sign. She knows I will not go with her – but I think she is assuming my continued existence even if I do not. Both she and I are expected to survive the separation.

Josephine has improved noticeably in her behaviour at the Unit. She is much more contained, she looks more mature, is sometimes thoughtful towards the other children, and her learning has increased rapidly. At home she is more manageable but boarding-school is still the realistic place for her because there is no suitable day-school. She provides a good example of someone for whom neither therapy, nor the therapeutic environment separately, could have effected the change that the two together have achieved. The constant repetition of interpretations about her anxieties while being held in an environment that was both understanding, and also authorative where necessary, somehow helped her constant experience of persecution to diminish. This abated and she was able to take in more and more what we could offer her, and to substitute expected good experiences for some of the bad ones. Her thoughts about boarding-school show that she still projects her own sadistic impulses into the unknown – the teachers who will cane her; but our hope is that if the teachers there are really, in her words, 'patient', i.e. if they can manage to contain the jumble of her anxieties and make sense of them, she will again be able to internalize real good experiences. Our hope is that she will be able to link her use of all of us at the Day Unit with this future experience.

NOTES

1 A version of this chapter was published in the *Journal of Child Psychotherapy* 9, 1983.
2 D. Daws, 'Child psychotherapy in a day unit', in D. Daws and M. Boston (eds) *The Child Psychotherapist*, Wildwood House, 1977.

Fees for this Chapter have gone to the Child Psychotherapy Trust, 27 Ulysses Road, London NW6 1ED
The Trust is dedicated both to making treatment widely available to children and families with emotional problems, and to ensuring that more child psychotherapists are trained to work in the N.H.S.

Chapter Eight

WORKING WITH THE FAMILIES OF CHILDREN WITH EMOTIONAL AND BEHAVIOURAL DIFFICULTIES

GILLIAN MILES

The family is central to the world of the child and to his[1] sense of identity. It is within families that the first attachment relationships are made, and patterns set for later life, whether these patterns are good or bad. In understanding children with emotional and behavioural difficulties, therefore, it is vital to think about the child in the context of the family, and thinking about families must be done when planning treatment and management strategies if these plans are to succeed.

However, over recent years the structure of the family in our society has changed. The significant increase in marital breakdown means that now about one in four families has only one parent, and many children find themselves in reconstituted families. There is less stability in family life, and a greater awareness and concern in society about family violence and child abuse. The greater prevalence of unemployment also has its impact on the family. A child with difficulties may well have a family under stress.

Just as there is a wide range of problems with which families can present, there is a range of professionals and agencies to help children and families. Difficulties may be apparent in early childhood, and brought to the doctor or health visitor, or noticed in the nursery. Teachers may become aware of the child's difficulties in school, or parents themselves, aware of difficulties at home, realize that they need help. What help is available depends on the services in any particular area. In some places there are few specialist services, and the brunt of the work falls on the NHS primary care workers, the Social Services, the schools, the educational social worker, and the local educational psychologist. In other places, however, there are specialist services, special units, and teams set up for families under stress, and a Child and Family Mental Health Clinic. Since these clinics have played a major part in the assessment and treatment of emotionally disturbed children, I propose to consider family assessment from the viewpoint of the clinic and the multidisciplinary team.

Within the clinic the different team members bring their particular skills and knowledge, and their professional links with colleagues in the community. The combination of the contributions of the child psychiatrist, the psychologist, social worker, and in some teams the child psychotherapist, remedial teacher, nurse, and occupational therapist, in approaching families and their problems, brings together facets which contribute to a fuller picture of the child, the family, and his world. Teams can have many different approaches, but whatever the approach, it seems to me that there is a need to compile a family history, including an account of the child and his development in the context of his family.

Thinking together with parents about the family history is a way of getting to know them, and establishing a relationship which contains enough trust to continue to work together, particularly when painful intervention is needed. Parents often have an intense sense of guilt and failure about their child's difficulties and problems. They have concerns about the possibility of labelling for the future of their child. Again, thinking about the past often evokes painful memories, which must be faced when thinking about links with present problems.

The family history sets the present problems in the context of the histories of all the significant family members, and the relationships between them. Detailed thought is given to the child, his present difficulties, and how they have developed over the years, and a general history of his development. Alongside, a picture is built up of the parents and siblings, and of the family in its environment. In learning about the parents and their backgrounds, and how they have struggled with difficulties in the past, it is possible to get some sense of their capacities to cope in the present. Attitudes towards children emerge, and some idea of parenting capacity. If parents are totally submerged in their own battles over a divorce, for example, there may be little room for thought about the children. This may be a temporary state of affairs, or it may be reflected throughout the child's life. Patterns may emerge in the history which reflect repetitions across the generations, and throw light on the question of why this child has these difficulties now.

Strengths and weaknesses become clear within the family, together with indications of the family's openness to intervention and change. The assessment is made by bringing together the contributions of the team members, from the child's point of view, from the parent's point of view, and what is known of the concerns of the outside world. Once a thorough assessment is made, then possibilities of intervention can be considered.

Different conceptual theories lead to different strategies of intervention. A systemic approach, for example, would take as its primary focus the system of relationships within the family and the network surrounding it. A behavioural approach would be centrally concerned with behavioural symptoms, and intervention towards behavioural change. In my examples, my approach is from a psychodynamic orientation, thinking centrally about individuals, against the background of the past and the possibility of the repetition of unconscious patterns. In practice, no one approach excludes the others; one can inform the other, or be appropriate in one situation rather than another.

Assessment is important, because of the wide range of problems and difficulties that exist, both in the children and the families. At one extreme, there are profoundly damaged and disturbed children, with psychosis or autism, physical illness or brain damage. The behaviour of the child may be bizarre, and the stress on the family very great. Nevertheless, the family may function well and be able to provide a good enough environment, even at a cost (and the effect of such children on their siblings merits consideration). Other children may have severe behavioural disturbances, but also be living in damaged, splintered families where parenting capacity is limited, parents are overwhelmed by their own problems, and have little space for their children and their needs. Yet others have severe difficulties, the families have difficulties, but also intrinsic strengths, which can be mobilized by intervention. The range is from healthy families struggling with the effects of trauma and neurotic difficulties, to grossly disturbed families with little capacity to cope.

The outcome of assessment leads to hypotheses about the problem, the family and its dynamics, and the most helpful form of intervention for both the child and the family. There is a wide range of possible interventions, which will be considered under the following headings:

139

1. Therapeutic intervention:
(a) Intervention with the family leads to improvement, so the child stays in normal school, with a lessening of the problems.
(b) Treatment for both child and family leads to improvement and the child remains at normal school.
(c) Child placed in special school, while parents are supported.
(d) Child placed in special school and parents supported so that the placement is not sabotaged.

2. Management intervention:
(e) Child goes to boarding-school.
(f) Placement in special boarding-school, child needing special help and a therapeutic environment.
(g) Child goes to special boarding-school following legal intervention.
(h) Child needs immediate removal to foster care.
(i) No legal grounds for intervention, parents refuse intervention, and professionals must wait for the situation to break down.
(j) Early intervention and preventive work.

This spectrum can best be illustrated by examples of children and families whom I have seen in a clinical setting.

THERAPEUTIC INTERVENTION

(a) **Intervention with the family leads to improvement, so the child stays in normal school, with a lessening of the problems.**

Example:
Ben, aged 10, was referred by his school. An able boy, he had become unable to concentrate, did not want to go to school, and was very distressed and tearful. The school was aware that there had been problems at home and that the parents had separated.

Ben's mother came on her own for a first meeting. She was severely depressed and tearful, and explained that the whole family had been traumatized by the break up of the marriage. Her elder children, David aged 12 and Sarah aged 16 seemed to be managing, but Ben had taken it very hard. He was depressed at home, and finding the access visits to his father very difficult. He had been very close to both parents, neither of whom could communicate directly with the other since father had left the family. Mother was finding it difficult to get through to Ben herself, and was concerned by the extent of his depression. The family had not had previous problems.

Our hypothesis following this meeting was that communication within the family had broken down, and that it was important to see Ben's difficulties within the framework of the family. We invited the whole family, including father, to a meeting. This was father's first meeting with the family since his departure, and proved a very painful occasion. Of the three children, Ben was most clearly distressed, and began by being spokesman for all three. Gradually, however, over the course of a series of meetings, Sarah and David were able to recognize the extent to which he was taking responsibility for the whole family's pain, and were more able to acknowledge their own share in it. The parents realized that they could not leave the burden of communication between them on Ben's shoulders. The anger, hurt, and pain were acute for them all, but this intervention freed Ben, who became noticeably less depressed, and able to get back to school and concentrate on school work. Mother recognized her need for help for herself, thus freeing all the children to handle their own feelings and loyalties.

This family had sufficient strength to cope with the trauma, and despite their own distress, both parents had concern for the children, and capacity to act as parents.

(b) **Treatment for both child and family leads to improvement and the child remains at normal school.**

Example:

Colin, aged 6, was referred by his parents. His explosive behaviour at home was almost impossible for them to handle, and the family was dominated by his rages. At school he was very disruptive in his class, and unable to concentrate. The school was getting to the end of its tether, and near to excluding him. The referral had been triggered by a very worrying accident, the latest in a series of self-destructive events when Colin had been in danger of hurting himself very badly. There were two older children, both of whom seemed to be doing well, at home and at school.

Colin's parents were both caring and extremely concerned, and unable to give any explanation for his behaviour. His difficult behaviour dated back to his second year, and they had speculated about its origin. Thinking about the family history, it emerged that during that year mother's father had died. As she talked about her own childhood, it became clear that she had had a very ambivalent relationship with her father, who was an unpredictable person with a violent temper, and that at the time she had been badly shaken, and unable to mourn his death. Instead she and Colin had become very close, and this relationship had not changed, despite him getting older. His rages were difficult for both parents to control; both, it seemed, had had parents with violent tempers, and the problems they experienced with Colin seemed linked with their own past experiences.

We felt that both Colin and his parents could be helped by individual psychotherapy. Meanwhile, the psychologist visited the school and discussed Colin's behaviour at school, in the attempt to hold Colin within a normal class setting.

Treatment plans were set up, with Colin seeing a child psychotherapist for weekly sessions, while mother or both parents came for their own sessions. Besides thinking about the problems with Colin, and her relationship with him, mother used the time to rethink her own childhood, tracing her relationships with her own parents. This thinking had been suspended when her father had died, because it was too painful, and even now it proved very difficult. She began to realize the close links between their difficulties in handling Colin's rages, and the past, when her own intense rage had only had room for expression in her imagination. Meanwhile, there were parallel themes in Colin's therapy, as he struggled with the problems of his inappropriately omnipotent behaviour. The closeness of the relationship between mother and child was mirrored by the similar themes and images they brought to their sessions. Both parents meeting together thought about their lack of confidence in handling Colin's rages, and change slowly occurred. The school reported a great improvement in Colin: he was more able to work, other children were less frightened of him, and he was beginning to make friends. His mother, for her part, felt relieved that he had a life of his own, and she was able to think more about her other children, whose difficulties had been masked because their brother had been the central problem and had monopolized all the attention.

This family had strengths and the capacity for change, and could use psychotherapy. Without this intervention, there was little doubt that Colin's problems at school would have continued, and he would have needed special schooling.

(c) Child placed in special school, while parents are supported.

Example:

Peter, aged 8, was referred by the school, which was very concerned by his uncontained behaviour. He was a cheeky but likeable boy, who was unable to settle in class, constantly running out and disappearing for long periods of time. There were instances of petty thieving, and he had been picked up by the police. The school felt concerned that the parents were not in control, and worried about Peter's welfare and safety.

When Peter and his parents came to the clinic, it was soon clear that this was a very deprived family, struggling to manage. Peter was the only child. Both parents had had difficult, deprived childhoods, and mother had suffered all her life with emotional problems, as well as debilitating physical illness. She had herself had special schooling as a child. Both parents were immature, and had difficulty managing their own lives, work, and financial problems. There were severe marital tensions, and little space available to consider Peter's needs. They spoke of their own difficulties in controlling Peter, his bouts of stealing both at home and from local shops, and of his preoccupation with matches and with fire. They were fond of Peter, and needed him; Peter often looked after his mother when she was ill. However, they had little parenting capacity, and there seemed little prospect of change.

We recommended that Peter should go to a special school where he could be a weekly boarder. Peter's parents found this decision difficult to accept, and work was done with them to recognize that he needed special help with his difficulties. Once Peter was at the school, his parents were seen regularly by the school social worker, who maintained a liaison between them and the teaching staff, and supported them in their care of him at weekends and during holidays.

There was little hope for change with these very immature, dependent parents, and therefore the best that could be offered was alternative care for Peter, and support for his parents to maintain their role as parents and links with the school.

(d) **Child placed in special school and parents supported so that the placement is not sabotaged.**

Example:

Graham, aged 10, was referred to the clinic by his teacher at school. For a long time he had found school difficult, and he had had several changes of school. The situation had deteriorated to such a degree that for the last term he had not been into class except for the occasional lesson, and he had spent most of the time in the teacher's office. With a change of school pending, the situation would not be able to continue, and intervention was needed.

Although they were no longer together, Graham's parents came together with him to the clinic. They were both very anxious about Graham's difficulties and his behaviour at home and at school. As they told the family history a picture emerged of a very ill child, struggling to hold on to a sense of reality. He was unable to work, he could not relate to other children, and he had severe obsessional rituals.

The parents were themselves very anxious, and concerned that Graham should have therapeutic help. However, neither of them could face the implications in reality for his schooling, and had quite unrealistic expectations that he could go on to the senior school of their choice, a large comprehensive school. Given the extent of his problems, it was quite clear that this could not work, but the parents were so determined that it was important that they should find out for themselves that it was not possible. Consequently, we left the school negotiations in their hands, while arranging psychotherapy for Graham, and joint work with the parents to think about their parenting roles.

Inevitably the chosen school could not consider Graham, and the parents turned to the clinic for help. The psychologist found a small Special Unit which could provide both the therapeutic environment in which Graham could manage, and the teaching which he needed. Both parents found these plans difficult to accept, concerned that Graham would lose touch with the normal school system and normal children, and that his education would fall behind. They had unrealistic aspirations for his education, and felt guilty about what they saw as their failure as parents.

A great deal of work was done to support the placement, and to enable Graham to stay there for the next 2 years. Graham's complaints at home about the Unit upset his parents, who joined in criticizing the staff, and needed to be reminded of Graham's own difficulties. Meanwhile, Graham's therapist worked directly with Graham around his difficulties in the Unit, and the psychologist liaised with the staff to enable them to tolerate and understand the pressures of his rejecting behaviour on them and the attitude of his parents.

Throughout this time, it was crucially important to maintain good communication between all the professionals who were involved with the family, to avoid them being set against one another. Collusion with Graham's complaints could have led to breakdown of the placement, rather than giving him a chance to master his difficulties. The attacks on professional links in such situations can be very powerful, reflecting the family's own difficulties, and making it difficult for professionals to work together unless they understand the splitting and projection that are taking place.

MANAGEMENT INTERVENTION

Management intervention becomes necessary when at assessment it seems very unlikely that change can be effected by therapeutic intervention alone, and it is in the interests of the child to be away from home. There are a variety of reasons for taking this decision. The child may need therapeutic help only available in a total environment; he may be caught in a web of family conflicts which are harmful to his development, or, in extreme situations, felt to be at risk through lack of care.

Professionals are involved with the parents in the making of these decisions, with which they may or may not agree, or find very painful. Once the child is away, links between home and school are maintained, sometimes still involving the assessment team, but sometimes resting more with the staff of the residential establishment. These links vary in intensity, but again become more important when the time approaches for the child to leave school.

(e) Child goes to boarding school.

Example:

James, aged 9, was referred by the school. He was seen as a worried child, who could not settle to work, and who was bullying other children. At home his behaviour was difficult, with explosive temper outbursts and occasional encopresis.

At the assessment we found an extremely tense home situation. Although James's parents were divorced, they were locked in continuing battles, which now that they were apart, centred on access arrangements and the care of the children. Both were vulnerable people; both felt that the other was being unreasonable, and these battles often took them to Court. James's position was impossible, with loyalties to both parents. He was an intelligent child, who was disabled in his learning by his anxieties.

Although the parents were unable to be in the same room with each other, separately both could see that it would be in James's best interests to go away to school. They were able to make these arrangements themselves with the backing of the clinic. James's housemaster was alerted to the problems, and counselling was provided at the school. The clinic staff remained available to the parents, particularly at times of crisis between them, and with regular appointments in the holidays. It took James time to settle, but gradually his symptoms lessened, and he began to work to his potential.

Both James and his mother were relieved of stress, though the family problems remained. There was some concern for James's brother, a very withdrawn child, who remained at home.

(f) Placement in special boarding-school, child needing special help and a therapeutic environment.

Example:

John, aged 12, was referred by his mother because he was severely depressed, and suicidal. The family was very frightened, could not cope, and felt they had reached the end of their resources.

At the assessment John was felt to be at risk because of his severe depression. The family history showed his problems to be of very long standing. He had never coped with the world outside his home, and within it, the family were dominated by his moods. His mother felt trapped by his depression, and although his elder siblings were protective towards him, they needed to get on with their own lives. Given the extent of John's illness, family work was not felt to be appropriate, as he needed special care and a safe environment which his family could not provide.

The family was relieved when John was placed in a residential therapeutic community school. Without the pressure of his full-time care, they were far more able to respond to him on his visits home. John himself was relieved of pressures to succeed, and found greater self-esteem within a setting where he could achieve. John's parents were relieved, but also distressed. Work was done with them at the clinic over a period of time, enabling them to reflect on John's difficulties, his position in the family, their own depression reactivated by his behaviour, the management of his weekend visits home, and their relationship with the school.

In both these examples, parents were able to think towards plans which were in the best interests of their child, and to work alongside the professionals involved. The decisions they had to make were painful, but they had the parenting capacity to hold the child and his needs in mind. In other situations, however, this is not the case, and professionals are forced to intervene.

(g) **Child goes to special boarding-school following legal intervention.**

Example:

Ruth, aged 13, a ward of court, was referred to the clinic by the local Social Services Department for a second opinion and report to the Court because of its intense concern for Ruth's welfare. There had been concern about Ruth for some time, but all attempts at therapeutic intervention had been blocked by the parents. We were being asked to assess whether this family could use therapeutic help.

The concern was that Ruth was seen as the scapegoat in her family. She was the eldest child, and the allegations were that she was singled out for particularly harsh treatment. These allegations, if true, rightly concerned the professionals. There had been a crisis when she had been taken into care on a voluntary basis. The parents had been very angry and distressed, and since then had refused all help, saying that matters had improved.

The parents agreed to an independent assessment, knowing that this would involve a report to the Court. The whole family was seen, including Ruth's younger siblings. We experienced the parents' fury with the other professionals. However, we were also very concerned by Ruth's position, and felt that she was a child at risk in her family, with a history of tensions and difficulties starting early on in her life. Her parents, both deprived people themselves, showed little capacity for insight and change, and hopes for Ruth in her adolescence rested, in our opinion, on her removal from home into a residential therapeutic setting.

Ruth's parents did not want to let her go. However, they recognized the power of the Court to intervene and did not fight our recommendation. The acknowledgement of the difficulties that they had both experienced in their own childhoods and their early marriage helped to alleviate their sense of guilt and failure in their parenting of Ruth. Once that was acknowledged, they were more free to think about her needs.

An important aspect of this case was, again, the communication between the professionals involved with the family – the social workers, the school, the local clinic, and ourselves. Ruth's situation had provoked very strong and divergent opinions and conflict between them, making it difficult to reach a decision. It was necessary for the professionals to meet to think about this conflict and understand what it reflected of the family's problems, before Ruth's needs could really be considered.

(h) **Child needs immediate removal to foster care**.

Example:

Anne, aged 4, was referred by the Health Visitor. She had been in foster care for 18 months, following the breakup of her parents' marriage, and her mother's subsequent physical and emotional abuse towards her while they had been living in a Women's Refuge. Now the Social Services were planning to return Anne to her mother Paula. The Health Visitor was anxious about this, knowing that Paula's access visits to the foster home were very difficult, and that Anne could be very provocative and difficult. When her demands were not met she would sometimes smear faeces, or annoy her foster mother by hiding away things that were vital for the running of the home. She could also be very jealous of the foster mother's own small children, and was not an easy child to look after.

After consultation with the other professionals involved, we saw Anne and her mother for assessment. Anne was a superficially bright, attractive, and charming child, showing premature ego development, but under her façade she was very deprived, preoccupied with violence, and anxious about her mother. Mother was herself a deprived and immature young woman with little self-esteem. She had married while still in her teens to a violent young man, who had himself been brought up in an institution. Throughout Anne's early life the couple had had no stability, and continual violent rows: after one of these Paula had tried to kill herself. Her own childhood had been dominated by a violent father, and her own violence towards Anne had erupted when she had seen her trying to strangle another child in the Refuge, behaviour which reminded her of her own father's behaviour.

Now that permanent plans had to be made for the future, Paula wanted to make a new start and to have Anne back to live with her. The Social Services were prepared to help by providing accommodation. Our concern mirrored that of the foster mother. Paula was depressed, had no stable life or relationships, moving promiscuously from one unsatisfactory relationship to another, and had little realistic idea about how to handle Anne. We suggested that time was needed for a longer period of assessment and preparation, and that during this time Anne and her mother should make regular visits to the clinic, to think about the difficulties for them both. In her sessions, Paula was very open and honest about herself, her temper and her impulsiveness, her loneliness and her need for support. She made regular visits to care for Anne in the foster home, and although at first she had been impatient to have her home straight away, she became more thoughtful about Anne's provocative behaviour and her needs, and about the problems she herself experienced in controlling Anne, because she was frightened of losing her temper.

During this time she became less depressed, got herself a job, and formed a stable relationship with a young man who seemed to care for both her and Anne, and to be aware of Anne's problems. At one of the regular review meetings of all the professionals, including the foster mother, it was agreed that the situation had improved sufficiently to let Anne go home to her mother, under close supervision from the Social Services, and keeping a watchful eye on Anne in school.

While the clinic was working with Paula and Anne, a specialist social worker was supporting the foster mother in her very taxing role. Although she was experienced, she found the combination of Anne's difficult behaviour and Paula's demands very stressful at times, besides her concern for her own children, who had to cope with Anne's jealous behaviour, and the often stormy aftermath of Paula's visits. In addition, like many other short-term foster mothers she had in fact found herself in a long-term situation of caring for Anne, which placed far greater emotional strains on her and her family.

(i) **No legal grounds for intervention, parents refuse intervention, and professionals must wait for the situation to break down.**

It is not hard to understand that these are amongst the most painful situations for the professional worker, who is forced into a position of inactivity, knowing that the child's needs are not being met, or that the position of the child is potentially very damaging. The most that can be done is to ensure that the professionals involved are aware of the anxiety surrounding the family, in touch with each other, and ready to use any opportunity that arises for intervention.

Example:

There had been acute concern about Kate, aged five, and her younger sister Jane, aged ten months, living with their very damaged and immature mother and her boyfriend. Kate had already been in care, following severe neglect by her mother. The care arrangements had broken down, and there had been insufficient evidence to prevent Kate returning to her mother at her request.

The situation was again deteriorating. The Health Visitor, who had access to the home, could see the baby's apathy and distress and the inadequacy of the emotional and physical care of both children. The social worker was denied access to the home, and was concerned, but did not feel there were sufficient grounds for intervention. All the professionals involved, and there were many, were forced into inactivity, reliant on the Health Visitor's reports that things had not deteriorated further, and the school's surveillance of Kate. Action was only possible when the mother left the home, abandoning the children, who were then taken into care. Again, a great deal of work had gone on among the professionals, at meetings and Case Conferences, holding together anxiety and different points of view.

(j) **Early intervention and preventive work.**

Jane and Kate's predicament leaves a very bleak picture of the possible extent of the neglect of children who are already in difficulties. Whereas we know that no amount of early intervention could have helped their mother, who was not open to change, it seems important to end by emphasizing the possible role of early intervention with the families of young children.

Example:

Nicholas, aged 2½, was referred to the clinic by the Health Visitor, who was concerned about both mother and child's clear distress. Nicholas was constantly waking in the night in a distressed state and disturbing his parents' sleep. He was also acutely upset whenever his mother attempted to leave him with anyone else, even for short periods of time.

Nicholas's parents brought him to the clinic. He was a very sensitive child, showing intense concern for his mother, and he was unable to let her out of his sight. Interviews with the parents left us concerned about the marriage, and about mother's depression, which had begun after Nicholas's birth. There seemed to be no clear boundaries between the child and his parents' problems.

Intervention focused on the parents, their anxieties and difficulties. Mother felt greatly relieved, in her regular meetings, to be able to share her depression and think about it, and the problems in the marriage began to be addressed. The parents became more aware of the burdens that Nicholas had been carrying, and were therefore more able to protect him from them. He was soon able to go to nursery school, though it was some time before his sleep disturbance improved.

CONCLUSION

These examples, taken from a clinic setting, and from the viewpoint of the social-work role within the multidisciplinary team, set out to show the wide range of families with children with emotional and behavioural difficulties. When decisions have to be made about appropriate provision, therefore, I have stressed the need for careful assessment. Most of the assessments described took place over a period of time, giving time for thought and the review of first impressions in the light of greater knowledge of the families.

We have also relied heavily on two key factors when a choice had to be made between working with a family and opting for special placement or residential care for a child. The first was an individual assessment of the child, his internal world, and his individual needs. The second was the family history, given by the parents or the family, giving thought to the child's position in the family, and the parenting capacity of the parents. Of prime importance was the experience of parenting that the parents had had themselves, and their capacity for insight and change. This information formed the basis for making choices of intervention; for example, whether there was sufficient support for treatment to take place within the family, or not.

In several of the examples there has been concern for siblings, preoccupied as parents have been with the more severely disturbed child in the family. In each instance when treatment was offered, it was noticeable that improvement in the child allowed the parents to be more aware of difficulties being experienced by other children in the family – for example, problems with school or peer relationships. These difficulties had often been present for some time, but the central stress in the family left little room for them to be noticed. These are often the normal difficulties of growing up, but there are occasions when siblings are under considerable stress, and need help in their own right.

When children are placed in special schools, a great deal of work is often done both in supporting the families, and in maintaining the links with the child and the school. This work is sometimes done by social workers, sometimes by the teaching staff in the schools, using many different theoretical approaches.[2] The social-work role in the setting of a special school or unit also involves working with a network of other professionals involved with the family.

I have given several examples of the complex and difficult roles carried by the professional in working with the more severely disturbed families, when often there are many professionals involved. The family's own conflicts and uncontained primitive feelings can very easily get reflected in the professional network, with different workers taking up different positions, and re-enacting the conflict.[3] In addition, there are inevitably interprofessional conflicts and rivalries, or confusions and rivalries about the various roles professionals hold in working with a particular family. Roles need to be clearly defined, and underlying conflicts understood and worked with, if the network is going to succeed in focusing on the family and the task of helpful intervention.[4-6]

Working with such families involves surviving the impact of very painful feelings, both in direct work with the families and in working within the professional network. In particular, management decisions which cut across family patterns and defences inevitably cause pain and arouse opposition and resistance. The professional network can be of great value in containing anxiety and giving space for thought, when there is sufficient trust to work with the conflicts that arise. It is equally essential that the families can trust the professionals to listen, consider their feelings, and think in their best interests.

NOTES

1 For convenience, I use 'his' whenever referring to the child, rather than 'his/her'.
2 See various articles in the journal *Maladjustment and Therapeutic Education*, the Journal of the Association of Workers for Maladjusted Children, 1986 and 1987.
3 R. Britton, 'Breakdown and reconstitution of the family circle', in M. Boston and R. Szur (eds) *Psychotherapy with Severely Deprived Children*, London: Routledge & Kegan Paul, 1983.
4 J. Hutten, 'Thinking together about children in care', in M. Boston and R. Szur (eds) *Psychotherapy with Severely Deprived Children*, London: Routledge & Kegan Paul, 1983.
5 Christine Hallett and Olive Stevenson, *Child Abuse: Aspects of Interprofessional Co-operation*, London: George Allen & Unwin, 1980.
6 Lesley Holditch, 'Bridge building between teachers and social workers', in E. Dowling and E. Osborne (eds) *The Family and the School: A Joint Systems Approach to Problems with Children*, London: Routledge & Kegan Paul, 1985.

Chapter Nine

THE MANAGEMENT OF CHILDREN WITH EMOTIONAL AND BEHAVIOURAL DIFFICULTIES IN ORDINARY AND SPECIAL SCHOOLS

COLIN J. SMITH

What do we mean when we talk about children with emotional and behaviour difficulties? Too often this important question leads to an attempt to define the children themselves, when time and attention would be better directed towards defining their difficulties.

Understanding the causes of problems in learning and adjustment is as important to teachers as it is to other workers with disturbed youngsters. However, as far as classroom management is concerned, it is essential to avoid any assumption that there is a certain 'type' of child who presents difficulties with regard to feelings, impulses, and the formation and maintenance of relationships. It is very easy in discussing special educational needs to concentrate too much on what is special or different about children rather than on what should be special or different about the way in which they are taught.

Management can be seen as a continuing process of assessment and intervention through which teachers discover whether or not children can be helped in a particular setting. Sometimes this may indicate the merits of moving a pupil from an ordinary to a special school but this should be because the special school is able to provide facilities or an educational regime which is not available within the ordinary school. It should not be a judgement about whether the child is bad enough but whether the school is good enough!

This approach does not seek to deny the often complex aetiology of emotional and behaviour disorders. As the Warnock Report[1] points out, such disorders may have many causes, including difficult home circumstances, adverse temperamental characteristics, and brain dysfunction. However, many problems do derive from the environment rather than from within the individual. Indeed, part of the Warnock Report's argument for retaining the use of the word 'maladjustment' as a serviceable descriptive term, though not as a categorical definition of disability, was that it carried the implication that 'behaviour can sometimes be meaningfully considered only in relation to the circumstances in which it occurs'.

If the child's needs can be met and problems solved by changing the way in which the school deals with that pupil, then the issue of whether to apply the label of 'maladjustment' or 'emotional and behaviour difficulties' should not arise. If, however, the necessary provision is beyond the resources of the ordinary school or if behaviour continues to cause concern despite alterations to methods of teaching and support, then the question of whether a different environment would help does arise. Yet this should still not be a matter of deciding the appropriate diagnostic label.

The 1981 Education Act and the attendant circulars advising on its implementation suggest that assessment of special educational needs should be a process of observation, discussion, and negotiation, involving parents as well as a variety of professionals. This process should determine whether a pupil's special needs are sufficiently severe or complex to merit the protection of a formal written statement. Even where this is necessary, the emphasis should be on defining what is required in the way of specialist teaching, facilities, or equipment to enable access to the normal school curriculum. In practice, what has come to be known by the ugly, clumsy, and depersonalizing term 'statementing' is little different from previous administrative procedure which 'ascertained' that a child belonged to a particular category of handicap.[2]

In relation to emotional and behaviour difficulties, this means that there is still a tendency for assessment to dwell on the inadequacies of the individual instead of examining possible adaptations to the school's methods of dealing with problems. Possibly with a sincere belief that removal will be best for all concerned, there may be a reluctance to try altered approaches for fear that the school will be left with a problem, which it might otherwise avoid. Unfortunately, the capacity and willingness to cope with difficult children does not rate as highly as it should in the assessment of a school's performance. Yet there is evidence to suggest that there is no contradiction between meeting the needs of children likely to be disaffected, disruptive, or maladjusted and maintaining good results in terms of high standards of attainment, attendance, and behaviour. Reviewing such evidence leads Galloway and Goodwin[3] to the conclusion that: 'The most effective procedures for preventing, rather than treating, disturbing or maladjusted behaviour are a by-product of processes which aim to raise the overall quality of education for *all* pupils in the school.' (Original emphasis)

These procedures relate to the ways in which schools are organized and the manner in which teachers respond to their pupils. Rutter *et al.*[4] identified three key features of the 'ethos' of successful schools: standards reflecting positive expectations, good models of teacher behaviour exhibiting commitment and concern, and effective feedback on what is acceptable conduct. When schools perform poorly in these areas they may well be contributing to problems traditionally explained in terms of the child's inadequacies. These undoubtedly play a part but they do not absolve the school from its responsibilities.

Where teachers have low expectations of their pupils it is not surprising that pupils react by living down to them. Evans[5] draws a distinction between 'insidious' and 'excessive' disruptive behaviour. The former is characterized by a climate which tolerates as commonplace lateness for lessons, failure to bring equipment or to produce homework, displays of open boredom, and unwillingness to concentrate on classroom tasks. Where this is the expectation of normal behaviour, it may foster more extreme actions, often associated with concepts of emotional and behaviour difficulties such as persistent aggression, serious damage to property, and violent attacks on pupils and staff.

Where teachers themselves provide a poor model of respect for the values which they are notionally trying to inculcate, pupils will take this as a cue for their own attitudes. If lessons start late and finish early, if work is not marked, and anger turns rapidly to physical intervention, then pupils will be likely to adopt a similarly cavalier approach to punctuality and perseverance and an equally uncontrolled response to provocation. When children have already begun to copy inappropriate models outside school, as is often deemed to be the case with youngsters with emotional and behaviour difficulties, then once again the climate of the school will not create the problem but will certainly tend to exacerbate it.

Where pupils are unclear about acceptable boundaries for behaviour or about the likely consequences of their actions, then there is inevitable confusion. When feedback is not immediate and distinct, there is a tendency for children to see how far they can go, to see if there is a limit to outrageous behaviour or how little effort will be tolerated. For most children the point at which such limits are established will be readily discerned but maladjusted children described by Stott[6] as 'unable to act in their own best interests' will be likely to go too far in testing the system to destruction!

Prevention is better than cure and the first steps to meeting special educational needs are taken when good teaching in the ordinary school prevents a mild or moderate problem in learning and behaviour becoming more severe and complex. There will however be some cases where problems continue to arise even in schools which successfully meet the needs of most of their pupils. It is still important to retain a perspective which seeks to define the difficulties and look for methods of resolving them, rather than to diagnose the children and look for ways of removing them. This requires a series of responses which give opportunities for rational adjustment by the child to what are reasoned and reasonable expectations from the school.

Even if this process fails it should at the very least provide some indication of what sort of regime is more likely to succeed with a particular individual. In seeking to define an appropriate continuum of response, it is helpful to think in terms of three levels of intervention: classroom management, individual mediation, and behaviour modification. This is similar to the approach advocated by Hewett and Taylor[7] who suggest that there are three critical ingredients in any learning situation which form what they describe as the 'learning triangle'. These are the curriculum, the conditions of learning, and the consequences of behaviour. By examining and where necessary introducing changes in the tasks to be completed, the setting in which they work or the results which follow teachers can 'orchestrate' success for their pupils and develop harmony in the classroom.

MANAGEMENT AND THE CURRICULUM

Since categories of handicap are no longer defined, following the Education Act, 1981, the Department of Education and Science (DES) collects information about provision for pupils receiving special education on the basis of categories of curriculum need. The guidelines for different types of need are helpful in looking at what can be done to manage the problems of children with emotional and behaviour difficulties in ordinary and special schools.

'Mainstream plus support' is the term used to describe the situation in which individuals are given appropriate support to enable them to cope with the normal school curriculum. This support might take the form of specialist teaching, particular forms of organization, or additional resources, including ancillary help. Most schools should have an identified member of staff who is a specialist in teaching children with learning difficulties who will act as a 'support' teacher. This job combines the traditional skills of the remedial specialist in diagnosing and treating reading problems with a broader remit for adapting curriculum materials and co-operative team teaching to enable pupils to respond to the mainstream curriculum despite their difficulties. If a school does not have such a specialist, then help should be available through the local authority peripatetic learning support service. However, before looking for specialist help an examination of the curriculum may reveal problems in matching learning experiences to learning abilities.

Booth and Coulby[8] explore the links between the curriculum and pupil disaffection and disenchantment. They suggest that attitudes fostered by the overt and the covert 'hidden' curriculum may devalue pupils, their families, and their backgrounds. Decisions about streaming or setting or admission to certain examination courses may be construed as a message that the school has nothing much to offer an individual. That child's response may be to behave in ways which indicate that such feelings are reciprocated. As one boy memorably told Hargreaves,[9] one of his class-mates, by this stage in his school career renowned for his deviance and defiance in the C stream of the upper school, had started in the A stream and would have presented no disciplinary problems 'if only they had kept him clever!'

Many emotional and behaviour difficulties which schools experience with children might be avoided if the curriculum were so arranged that they were 'kept clever' by not being excluded from the normal range of school experiences. Nonetheless, many problems do arise because children often choose to ward off inadequacy by misbehaviour rather than acknowledge their own incompetence. It is as if they decide that it is better to be thought a nuisance than a numbskull! The best form of support for keeping such pupils within the mainstream may simply be the systematic scrutiny by individual teachers and by departments of the materials which they use and their suitability for mixed-ability teaching in terms of readability, subject-matter, style of presentation, and intellectual demands.

Access to the normal curriculum will often depend on adaptations in methods of response as well as choice of materials. Lunzer and Gardner[10] indicate a variety of alternatives to the overworked essay and comprehension exercises usually employed to test understanding of textbooks, and Cowie[11] shows how oral, visual, and dramatic activities can enliven topics for the less able child who might not be able to accommodate to the time-honoured lecture format used in teaching academic subjects.

If these features are adequately dealt with in the design of the mainstream curriculum then this will maintain what Weber[12] describes as the 'momentum' which comes from the pupils' realization that they have the capacity for achievement and the impetus and involvement that comes from the satisfaction of accomplishment. Some of the developments in the new General Certificate of Secondary Education examination courses, with an emphasis on coursework and projects rather than unseen papers, could be particularly useful in this respect. Assessment based on profiles of personal achievement and certification of short modules of learning experience are also beginning to become accepted methods of evaluation and these too should stimulate and retain interest and involvement for pupils easily discarded by the traditional system.

There will still be some pupils, though, who do require a curriculum which is different in kind as well as delivery.

'Modified curriculum' is the term used to describe what should be provided for children whose special educational needs would not be met properly by a mainstream curriculum. Although used by the DES in relation to children with moderate learning difficulties, it also provides an apt description of the curricular needs of some children with emotional and behaviour difficulties. Whilst every effort should still be made to integrate them within the mainstream there are different aspects of the curriculum, which may require particular emphasis. Laslett[13] suggests areas of the curriculum in which activities could help children towards adjustment.

Physical education can provide opportunities for increasing awareness of self-identity through concentration on bodily strengths and weaknesses. It will also aid motor co-ordination for children whose clumsiness may be a major part of their frustration with life. Games offer the experience of sharing and taking turns, practice in co-operation, and abiding by rules and of course an outlet for energy and aggression.

Drama, music, art, and craft are all subjects which combine creative and therapeutic experiences. Cookery is another area in which practical satisfaction can be found and literature through stories and poetry also has many therapeutic possibilities. In these areas pupils can find appropriate ways of expressing feelings, gain more insight into the feelings of others, and often establish their ability to perform well, thus enhancing their self-image. Remedial work on basic skills and planned and sustained teaching of social skills can also improve self-esteem.

Whilst these modifications may be possible within a mainstream setting it is more likely that a special school should be able to accommodate such emphases. Given a more flexible timetable and most probably more freedom from the dictates of the proposed national curriculum, it may well be that a major justification for the continued existence of special schools for pupils with emotional and behaviour difficulties could be their ability to demonstrate a capacity to provide a suitably therapeutic curriculum.

'Developmental curriculum' is the term used to describe what should be provided for children with severe learning difficulties. It involves the specification of sharply focused educational, social, and other experiences with precisely defined objectives and designed to encourage a measure of personal autonomy. This may be the appropriate approach for pupils with psychotic disorders whose conduct is so profoundly disturbed that normal development and educational progress is problematic if not impossible. Schizophrenic symptoms of hallucination and delusions or the extreme withdrawal into purposeless, repetitive activity of the autistic child may require a different perspective for curriculum planning.

Hewett and Taylor (see note 7) offer a classification of levels of learning competence which can help a teacher to identify links between difficulties in learning and characteristics often perceived as symptoms of emotional disturbance. They refer to basic competencies needed by all children if they are going to be successful learners. Rather like the way in which Freud's psychosexual stages identify tasks and experiences which affect the development of personality, these levels 'provide a developmental framework for describing emotional disturbance in learning and educational terms'. Again it should be stressed that many problems at each of these levels may be coped with in the normal setting and as part of normal lessons but for some pupils assessment of their performance at each level could prompt the development of an alternative curricular experience. The following suggestions taken from Hewett and Taylor are intended to be tried within the ordinary classroom, but with more serious problems it may be easier to accommodate them in special schools or classes. As with the therapeutic curriculum the necessity and effectiveness of a special educational environment might be judged to a large extent by its ability to adapt teaching and deploy resources to cope with these different levels of learning competence.

Attention problems, which amount to failure to make adequate contact with the environment, can be helped by reducing the distracting stimuli, presenting shorter discrete units of work, and an emphasis on concrete rather than abstract tasks.

Response problems occur where difficulties in verbal or physical co-ordination make it hard for pupils to participate. Communication can be encouraged by setting tasks which initially reduce criteria for correctness, guaranteeing some successful learning and gradually but systematically increasing inclusion in group activity.

Order tasks help children learn to adapt to routines and persevere with work until it is completed. They should reduce confusion and emphasize sequence and the importance of following directions and instructions. For some pupils this will mean providing very simple tasks so that restlessness and distractibility are supplanted by engagement and interest.

Exploratory tasks provide a wide range of experiences through which children are enabled to form realistic and accurate perceptions of the world. Disturbed children are often preoccupied with repetitive and sometimes fixated activities in one or two areas of the curriculum where they appear to find safety in familiarity. This can reinforce a very limited and distorted view of life in the classroom and beyond. Through art and science they can be introduced to new sensory experiences and to a more predictable environment.

Social tasks require skills in communication, adaptation, and co-operation in group work. Appropriate social behaviour may be learned through specific training programmes, modelling through positive peer interaction or practice at role-play. Drama has an evident importance in this area but other aspects of school life, particularly leisure and games experiences, have a lot to contribute. The careful organization of out-of-school visits, field trips, outings, and, as the child grows older, work experience will also be necessary.

Finally Hewett and Taylor consider the mastery level where skills relate to independence in self-care, academic learning, and vocational pursuits. Health, hygiene, and personal grooming may require particular training with some severely emotionally disturbed children, who may have little awareness of accepted expectations in these matters. Mastery of reading, writing, and computation skills, and preparation for employment, however, return attention to the essential normality of most youngsters with emotional and behaviour difficulties and the importance of trying wherever possible to provide for them in ordinary schools. Success will often depend as much on how schools plan the conditions and consequences of learning as it will on decisions about a suitable curriculum.

MEDIATION AND THE CONDITIONS OF LEARNING

Feuerstein[14] suggests that cognitive development depends on what he describes as 'mediated learning experience'. Children learn intelligent behaviour, he argues, through a combination of interaction with the environment and the interpretation of that experience through the intervention of an agent or mediator, who selects, filters, and directs attention to the important features of an event. In this way, children 'learn how to learn'. Through a series of structured activities described as Instrumental Enrichment, Feuerstein offers a teaching programme designed to enable teachers to act as mediators for retarded pupils.

The concept of the teacher as mediator has a wider application in relation to working with pupils with emotional and behaviour

162

difficulties. For these children, even when the content of teaching has been carefully selected, there is an additional need for the teaching environment to be arranged and interpreted with particular concern for the individual. The teacher acts in this sense as a mediator, by organizing the conditions of learning.

By examining the decisions they make about management, teachers can evolve strategies which reduce the potential for conflict and confrontation in the classroom. Not all pupils who are disruptive are emotionally disturbed but the problems of the latter will be exacerbated if the climate and atmosphere of the classroom is one of turmoil rather than tranquillity. Smith[15] outlines a framework for analysing classroom organization, indicating how teachers can identify aspects of the conditions of learning which may influence disruptive behaviour. This involves looking at the following features of classroom life: relationships, rules, and routines; assignments and rewards; working in groups; classroom design; and providing support.

Relationships, rules, and routines determine the emotional climate of the classroom. Just as in meteorology, the 'weather system' of the classroom is affected when minor disturbances build up into a larger area of turbulence. Successful classroom managers do not let petty misbehaviours develop in this way. Early intervention keeping attention focused on the work in hand is easier when pupils clearly understand the rules, which establish boundaries for acceptable behaviour and the routines, which regulate the flow of activities within the lesson. Good relationships depend on the personal interest shown by teachers in their pupils' welfare, but the opportunity to display that interest itself depends on effective and competent teaching. Whilst good teachers are often described in terms of personal characteristics and charisma, there are many tactics and techniques identified by research and observation which contribute to effective classroom management.[16]

Organization of assignments and rewards which is sufficiently considerate of differences in ability, aptitude, and motivation conveys positive expectations and provides encouragement. Tasks which are attainable, feedback from regular and informative marking, and the reward of social approval and praise for successful accomplishment ought to be standard features of the learning experience for all pupils. Too often, however, pupils with emotional and behaviour difficulties feel themselves to be excluded from any formal or informal reward system offered by the school. If teachers can find ways to maintain interest and motivation by making sure that such pupils do have a chance to succeed, then they will affirm belief in their potential to improve. As Weber (see note 12) puts it, encouragement is 'often the only tool a teacher has available when dealing with an adolescent in full retreat from learning'.

Working in groups is the first stage towards the more individualized approach which is such an essential aspect of the conditions of learning for any child with special educational needs. Dividing the class into smaller groups for at least some part of the time makes it easier for teachers to see children as individuals. The strengths and weaknesses of a particular pupil are much more visible when in a group of six or eight than when in a class of thirty or more. Groupwork also provides the basis for setting co-operative projects which can engage the withdrawn child in more social interaction and involve the disaffected youngster with others who offer a more positive model of behaviour.

If grouping is to be successful, then thought also has to be given to classroom design. This means considering the layout of desks, tables, and other furniture and resources. Sometimes, behaviour problems are much easier to control if pupils are sat at traditionally organized rows of desks. Certainly there will be more opportunity for distraction in less formal arrangements. However, it should be easier within group settings to make space available for 'quiet corners' and 'learning centres' where individuals can work on their own, if necessary, for some of the time. Waterhouse[17] discusses alternatives for classroom design and methods for solving associated problems in traffic control of movement round the room.

Providing support for individuals who are having problems involves the preparation and delivery of physical and human resources. Work should be allocated to groups so that they take turns at tasks which demand most teacher attention. Supplementary material should be ready to occupy 'waiting time' for groups or individuals who finish tasks more quickly than anticipated or who cannot get on with what they are doing until the teacher is available again. Lemlech[18] offers good examples of how to arrange learning centres to cope with this sort of problem. For many youngsters with difficulties in learning and behaviour, potential problems can be averted by having someone to whom they can turn for help and advice. Human support of this kind may be available from support teachers or other adult helpers or it may be provided by peer tutoring, perhaps pairing the less able child with a more able partner on what the Americans call the 'buddy system'.

Mediation also occurs through direct counselling and advice from the teacher. This type of intervention shifts the focus from conditions of learning to the consequences of behaviour.

MODIFICATION AND THE CONSEQUENCES OF BEHAVIOUR

Although it is unusual to think of counselling, associated as it is with humanistic psychology, in the same context as behaviourist approaches, both are methods which seek to change or modify behaviour by attending to its consequences. The counselling approach does this by reflection and revelation, the behaviourist by reward and reinforcement, but either way there is an emphasis on establishing links between cause and effect. Whatever the philosophical or ideological subtleties of the distinctions between the two theoretical standpoints, in helping children with emotional and behaviour difficulties teachers often use a combination of both.

Wolfgang and Glickman[19] suggest that there is a 'Teacher Behaviour Continuum' which stretches from non-interventionist to very firmly interventionist control techniques. At one end of this continuum, teachers use only supportive and accepting responses, aiming to help pupils work through their own misbehaviour. At the other end, teachers use commands, rewards, and punishments to correct misbehaviour. Once again the concept of a range of available possibilities offers a very useful perspective for examining how ordinary and special schools can respond to emotional and behaviour problems.

Wolfgang and Glickman argue that there are broadly three schools of thought about discipline in schools associated with psychoanalytic, social, and behavioural psychology.

The 'Relationship – Listening' school takes the view that the child develops from an inner unfolding of potential and that the job of education should be to provide a facilitating environment, which enables the expression of feelings. If there are difficulties in school then the teacher should have faith in the pupil's ability to wrestle with and solve problems. The teacher would counsel by listening, reflecting back feelings, avoiding judgement or direction, but trying to help the pupil take control of his or her own destiny.

The 'Confronting – Contracting' school takes the view that the child develops from the interaction of internal and external forces. Education should make pupils aware of behaviours that enhance or detract from social acceptability. If difficulties arise then the teacher should clarify and delineate boundaries, emphasizing the pupil's responsibility for finding a mutually acceptable solution. The teacher counsels by confronting children with the consequences of their actions and working out a plan or contract for improvement.

The 'Rules/Rewards – Punishment' school takes the view that the child's development is conditioned by external forces. Education should provide a controlled environment which shapes the social and academic skills required by society. If difficulties arise then it is the teacher's responsibility to find a solution by changing rewards or punishments so that the pupil's behaviour is modified.

Within the ordinary school it is possible to see these three approaches as broadly sequential. Obviously there will be times when physical danger to self or others must prompt an earlier resort to direct intervention but it is always best to try the easy way first. Assuming that the curriculum and the conditions of learning have already been examined, then the next line of enquiry should be the pupil's own self-awareness and self-esteem and these may best be investigated by counselling. The chance to talk through problems with a sympathetic adult who can offer comfort and reassurance may be all that some children need to redirect their own behaviour. Sometimes this is a chance denied by assumptions on the part of schools that nonconformists or rebels are invariably irrational. They may be incapable of acting in their own best interests but the question should always be asked whether they have been offered an opportunity to regain insight and self-control before more direct intervention is tried.

Where reflection has been tried and failed then more formal efforts can be made to demonstrate the consequences of continued antisocial behaviour. Much will depend on how effectively the school has organized its disciplinary system to provide a series of graduated sanctions and to record responses to them. Without resorting immediately to an elaborate programme of behaviour modification, there should be some process for identifying precisely what are the behaviours which are giving offence and what efforts have been made to alter them. This should produce the evidence on which to confront the child with the present unacceptable behaviour and the material for devising a suitable plan for its improvement. Part of this process should also involve gathering information not only about what has been done to discourage antisocial behaviour but also what more positive steps have been taken to reward more appropriate behaviour. All too often disciplinary systems are only concerned with stopping what is bad rather than promoting what is good.

If efforts to establish the give and take of normal social relationships through less formal methods are still failing, then at this stage, a more rigorous application of the behavourist approach could be the focus for a final attempt to cope with problems within the ordinary school. The first step of this approach would be the definition of precise behavioural 'targets' for observation and recording as a baseline of present behaviour. A programme of intervention to reduce undesirable behaviour and encourage more appropriate behaviour would then be introduced and monitored. An important factor in the success of such a programme will be the selection and delivery of appropriate rewards to reinforce desirable behaviours. It is sometimes claimed that within the conventional school system, it is not possible to offer sufficiently powerful rewards to affect the responses of seriously disturbed youngsters. This may be the case but this does not justify a failure to try an approach which has been used to good effect in ordinary schools.[20] If it has not succeeded then this may suggest that there is a need for a more specialized environment where it is easier to adopt and adapt an experimental regime.

It is not only with regard to the behaviourist approach that a special school may be a more suitable place to establish a radically different approach to education, particularly, though not necessarily exclusively, in residential situations. Wilson and Evans[21] describe a variety of treatments available in educational settings. Psychotherapy within a total living situation might range from free expression of instinctual impulses and the catharsis of 'acting out' to a deliberate strengthening of conscious control and contact with reality. Environmental or milieu therapy could offer family-type care with an emphasis on 'nurture' related to developmental level or there could be a regime based on the practice of self-government and shared responsibility. For schools which do subscribe to a behavourist approach the special school offers the opportunity of establishing a 'token economy'. This means that almost all behaviour can be shaped by awarding points, stars, or other tokens, which can be exchanged for rewards at a later time.

CONCLUSION

Few special schools do at present define their purpose and regime in a precise manner. With an increased emphasis on making provision within the mainstream whenever possible, there is likely to be an increasing pressure on segregated schools to justify their continued existence by showing exactly what they offer which cannot be made available within ordinary schools.

Special schools for pupils with emotional and behaviour difficulties may survive for the wrong reasons if ordinary schools are able to define problems in terms of the pupil's personality rather than their institutional provision. In some cases ordinary schools may be regrettably happy to abrogate their responsibility in this way. Similarly, some special schools may be unfortunately complacent about sustaining numbers without sufficient regard to suitability of placement. However, the vast majority of schools, both ordinary and special, are concerned with making the best arrangements they can for the management of emotional and behaviour difficulties. Following the triangular approach suggested here for the assessment of procedures for management, mediation and modification should ensure that a range of options is explored and that vital decisions are properly informed.

NOTES

1 DES *Special Educational Needs* (The Warnock Report), London: HMSO, 1978.
2 C. J. Smith, 'Let's stop "statementing" children', *British Journal of Special Education*, 12 (4) (1985).
3 D. Galloway and C. Goodwin, *The Education of Disturbing Children*, London: Longman, 1987.
4 M. Rutter, B. Maughan, P. Mortimore and J. Ouston, *Fifteen Thousand Hours; Secondary Schools and Their Effects on Children*, London: Open Books, 1979.
5 M. Evans, *Disruptive Pupils*, London: Schools Council, 1981.
6 D. H. Stott, *Delinquency: The Problem and its Prevention*, London: Batsford, 1982.

7 F. M. Hewett and F. D. Taylor, *The Emotionally Disturbed Child in the Classroom*, 2nd edn, Boston: Allyn & Bacon, 1980.
8 T. Booth and D. Coulby, *Producing and Reducing Disaffection*, London: Blackwell, 1987.
9 D. H. Hargreaves, *Social Relations in a Secondary School*, London: Routledge & Kegan Paul, 1967.
10 E. Lunzer and U. Gardner, *Learning from the Written Word*, Edinburgh: Oliver & Boyd, 1984.
11 E. Cowie, *History and the Slow Learning Child*, London: The Historical Association, 1979.
12 K. Weber, *The Teacher is the Key*, Milton Keynes: Open University Press, 1982.
13 R. B. Laslett, *Maladjusted Children in the Ordinary School*, Stratford-upon-Avon: National Council for Special Education, 1982.
14 R. Feuerstein, *Instrumental Enrichment*, Baltimore: University Park Press, 1980.
15 C. J. Smith, 'Analyzing classroom organization', in M. Scherer, L. Fry, and I. Gersch (eds) *Meeting Disruptive Behaviour*, London: Macmillan, in press.
16 R. B. Laslett and C. J. Smith, *Effective Classroom Management: A Teacher's Guide*, London: Croom Helm, 1984.
17 P. Waterhouse, *Managing the Learning Process*, London: McGraw-Hill, 1983.
18 J. K. Lemlech, *Classroom Management*, New York: Harper & Row, 1979.
19 C. H. Wolfgang and C. D. Glickman, *Solving Discipline Problems: Strategies for Classroom Teachers*, Boston: Allyn & Bacon, 1986.
20 K. Wheldall and F. Merrett, *Positive Teaching: The Behavioural Approach*, London: Allen & Unwin, 1984.
21 M. Wilson and M. Evans, *Education of Disturbed Pupils*, London: Methuen, 1980.

CONTRIBUTORS' ADDRESSES

Philip Barker
1820 Richmond Road SW
Calgary
Alberta
Canada T2T 5C7

Francis M. J. Dale
Child Guidance Clinic
8 Morgan Avenue
Torquay

Christopher Dare
18 Dacres Road
London SE23 2NW

Dilys Daws
The Tavistock Clinic
120 Belsize Lane
London NW3 5BA

Dr Robin Higgins
18 Park Road
E. Twickenham
Middlesex TW1 2PX

Dr David Jones
Department of Psychology
Birkbeck College, University of London
Malet Street
London WC1E 7HX

Gillian Miles
The Tavistock Clinic
120 Belsize Lane
London NW3 5BA

Jean E. Sambrooks
Department of Clinical Psychology
Royal Liverpool Children's Hospital
Alder Hey
Eaton Road
Liverpool L12 2AP

Colin J. Smith
Lecturer in Special Education
University of Birmingham
Ring Road North
P.O. Box 363
Birmingham B15 2TT

Ved P. Varma
27 Fryent Way
London NW9 9SL

NAME INDEX

Achenbach, T. M. 94, 95
Allen, L. 57
American Psychiatric Association 93
Aponte, H. 77
Arden, M. 16, 17

Bandler, R. 76, 77
Bandura, A. 57
Barker, P. 77
Barkley, R. A. 94
Benton, A. L. 94
Bion, W. R. 114
Booth, T. 169
Boston, M. 113
Bowlby, J. 39–40
Britton, R. 153

Cattell, R. B. 94
Chess, S. 78
Coan, R. W. 94
Cohen, S. 15
Conners, C. K. 94
Coulby, D. 169
Cowie, H. 169
Cox, A. 77

Dale, F. M. J. 113, 114
Dare, C. 39
Daws, D. 136
DiLeo, J. H. 77

Edwards, D. C. 94
Egert, D. 77
Elliott, C. 93
Evans, M. 168, 169

Evens, T. M. S. 17
Everitt, B. 77
Eysenck, H. J. 57
Eysenck, S. B. G. 94

Fairbairn, W. R. D. 39
Farley, G. K. 77
Feuerstein, R. 169
Fortes, M. 14
Fredman, G. 113
Freud, A. 39
Freud, S. 39
Frostig, M. 94

Galloway, D. 168
Gardner, U. 169
Gelfand, O. M. 57
Gillis, J. S. 94
Glickman, C. D. 169
Goffman, E. 16
Goodman, J. D. 77
Goodwin, C. 168
Goyette, C. H. 94
Graham, P. 77
Grinder, J. 76, 77

Hallett, C. 153
Hargreaves, D. H. 169
Hartman, D. P. 57
Hartmann, H. 39
Henderson, S. E. 94
Herbert, M. 57
Hersor, L. A. 16
Hewett, F. M. 169
Higgins, R. 15
Holbrook, D. 77

Holder, A. 39
Holditch, L. 153
Honzik, M. P. 57
Hopkinson, K. 77
Hutten, J. 153

James, W. 14
Johnson, A. M. 39
Jones, D. 94

Karper, M. A. 76
Kauffman, J. M. 57
Khan, M. M. R. 39
Klinedinst, J. K. 94
Kovacs, M. 94

Lacher, D. 94
Lang, M. 94
Laslett, R. 57
Laslett, R. B. 169
Lemlech, J. K. 169
Lunzer, E. 169
Lushene, R. E. 94

MacFarlane, J. W. 57
Matte Blanco, I. 14, 16
Maughan, B. 168
Merleau-Ponty, M. 14
Merrett, F. 169
Minuchin, S. 76
Montouri, J. 94
Mortimore, P. 168
Murray, D. J. 93

Neale, M. D. 93

O'Tuama, L. 95
Ouston, J. 168

Pearson, L. S. 93
Pincus, L. 39
Porter, R. B. 94

Report of the Underwood Committee 14
Routh, D. K. 95
Russell, B. 14
Rutter, M. 16, 77, 93, 94, 168

Ryle, G. 14

Sandler, J. J. 39
Satir, V. 76
Schacher, M. 93
Schonell, F. J. 93
Schroeder, C. S. 95
Seat, P. D. 94
Simmons, J. E. 77
Skinner, B. F. 57
Smirnoff, V. 39
Smith, A. 93
Smith, C. J. 168, 169
Sours, J. A. 77
Special Educational Needs Report 14
Spielberger, C. D. 94
Stevenson, O. 153
Stott, D. H. 95, 168
Strauss, E. S. 76
Szasz, T. 16
Szur, R. 113

Taylor, F. D. 169
Thomas, A. 77
Tisher, M. 94
Tizard, J. 16

Ulrich, R. F. 94

Varma, V. P. 77

Warnock Report 168
Waterhouse, P. 169
Weber, K. 169
Wechsler, D. 93
Wheldall, K. 169
Whitmore, K. 16
Wilson, M. 169
Winn, M. 14
Winnicott, D. W. 15, 39, 113, 114
Wirt, R. D. 94
Wittgenstein, L. 14
Wolfgang, C. H. 169
Wolpe, J. 57

Yule, W. 57

Zimet, K. J. 77

SUBJECT INDEX

anxiety in children: assessment of 89; behavioural treatment of 55–6, 89; *see also* fear in children
assessment: family 137–53; multidisciplinary 138, 139; in schools 159; *see also* behavioural assessment, cognitive assessment, intelligence tests, personality tests, psychiatric examinations
autism 103

behavioural approaches: to anxiety 55–6, 89; to assessment 90–2; assessment phase in 43–7; to child difficulties 41–57, 139, 165; increasing deficit behaviour 47–52; reinforcers in 47–52 *passim*; in schools 165, 167–8; shaping 50; social-learning theory 42, 47; therapeutic intervention in 47–57; 'time-outs' 53–4; token economy 168; weakening undesired behaviour 52–7
behavioural assessment 79, 90–2; rating scales (by parents) 91–2; rating scales (by teachers) 92
behavioural problems: attention span 49–50, 50–1; behavioural approaches to 41–57; circularity in 16n; clumsiness 87–8; defined 1–2; dressing 50; vs. emotional problems 1–2; and the family 137–53; learning difficulties 9–10, 81–4; and maladjustment 2–3; mealtime etiquette 49, 51; and personality assessment 88–9; planning for 11–14; psychiatric examinations for 58–78;

psychodynamic theory of 18–40; and school management 154–69; self-mutilation 43–4; temper tantrums 44; and therapeutic interventions 140–5; *see also* maladjustment

catharsis 27
cognitive assessment 79, 80–8; and clumsiness 87–8; and dyslexia 83; and hyperactive syndrome 85–8; inaccuracies in 82; of learning difficulties 81–4; of reading ability 84; and underachievement 84–5
counselling approaches: to child difficulties 165
countertransference 13, 107, 109

depression (childhood): treatment of 90
dreams: case-study 110–11; in psychiatric examinations 67
dyslexia 9, 83

education: *see* schools, special educational needs
Education Act (1944) 8
emotional problems: behavioural approaches to 41–57; vs. behavioural problems 1–2; defined 1; depression (childhood) 90; and the family 137–53; and maladjustment 2–3; parental expectations and 84–5; planning for 11–14; psychiatric examinations for 58–78; psychodynamic theory of 18–40; and school management 154–69; and therapeutic interventions 140–5; and

underachievement 84–5; *see also* maladjustment

families: abuse in 10–11, 19–24, 26–9, 31–2, 99–102; case-studies in intervention 140–51; history of 62–3; and intervention refusal 150; management intervention in 145–51; parental expectations in 84–5; preventive intervention in 150–1; psychiatric examinations of 59–65; therapeutic intervention in 140–5; working with 137–53
fear in children: behavioural approaches to 55–6; *see also* anxiety in children
foster care: case-study in 148–50
Freud, Anna 97; on child development 32–4; and ego-psychology 32–3
Freud, Sigmund 96–7; on childhood experience 25–32; on child sexuality 28–9, 31–2; clinical approach of 25–6; on drives 35; Oedipus complex 29; psychosexual stages 161; and resistance 118–19; *see also* psychoanalysis, psychoanalytic psychotherapy, psychodynamic theory

Handicapped Pupils and School Health Regulations (1945) 8–9
hyperactive syndrome 100; and cognitive assessment 85–8; DSM-III and 86

intelligence tests: critique of 80; in psychiatric examinations 72

Klein, Melanie 97; on child development 35–7; on child sexual knowledge 35–6; on developmental crises 36–7; on drive development 35; on object relations 36, 37; on paranoid-schizoid anxieties 36

learning difficulties 9–10; identification of 81–3; inaccurate assessment of 82; and psychological assessment 81–4; reading-ability tests 84; recognizing specific 83–4; spelling tests 84 *see also* dyslexia, intelligence tests, special educational needs
Lowenfeld, Margaret 97

maladjustment 1–6; and abuse 10–11; *vs* adjustment 6–8, 15n; context of 14–15n; and contrariety 6, 15n; counselling approaches to 165; identification of 11–14; index of 16n; and polarization 3–4; and scapegoating 4–5; Warnock Report on 155

Oedipus complex 29

parental expectations: and underachievement 84–5
personality tests: anxiety measurement in 89; for childhood depression 90; Children's Personality Questionnaire 89–90; and DSM-III 88; in psychiatric examinations 72; in psychological assessment 79, 88–90; questionnaires in 89–90
physical/sexual abuse 10–11; case-study in 19–24; familial cycle of 99–102, 113n; psychodynamic view of 26–7, 28–9, 31–2
psychiatric examination 58–78; assessment approaches to 67–73; case formulation in 73–6; child examination in 66–71; and children's dreams 67; defining goals in 61–2; of families 59–65; family history in 62–3; genograms in 63, 64; medical tests in 71, 72–3; non-verbal rapport in 60; physical examinations in 71; psychological tests in 72; records in 76; use of play/drawing in 68; verbal rapport in 60–1
psychoanalysis: nature of 24–5; *see also* Freud (Sigmund), Freud (Anna), psychoanalytic psychotherapy, Winnicott, D. W.
psychoanalytic psychotherapy 96–114, 117; abandonment and 103–5; adult *vs* child 97; case-studies in 102–5; child assessment in 102; containment/holding in 109; cure and termination in 112–13; cycle of deprivation and 99–102; and internal resources 102–6; interpretation in 109–12, 117; psychoanalytic relationship in 106–8; setting in 98; therapeutic skills in 108–12; transference in 106–8;

transgenerational re-enactment 101, 113n; treatment criteria in 99; use of play/drawing in 97–8; working through in 117; *see also* psychoanalysis, psychodynamic theory

psychodynamic theory: cartharsis 27; and child difficulties 18–40, 139; defences 33–4; ego 32, 33, 34; ego-psychology 32–3; id 32, 35; object relations 35, 36, 37; Oedipus complex 29; sublimation 34; superego 32; *see also* Freud (Anna), Freud (Sigmund), Klein (Melanie), psychoanalysis, psychoanalytic psychotherapy, Winnicott, D. W.

psychological assessment 79–95; behavioural assessment in 79, 90–2; cognitive assessment in 79, 80–8; critique of 80; justifications for 80; and learning difficulties 81–3; medical model in 80, 88; personality assessment in 88–90; in psychoanalytic psychotherapy 102; use of play/drawing in 68, 97–8

psychological tests: critique of 80; in psychiatric examinations 72; *see also* assessment

psychotherapy: case-study in institutional 127–36; case-studies in intervention 140–5; institutional aspects of 115–36 *passim*; institutional resistance to 118–19; psychoanalytic 96–114; teacher co-operation with 119, 120, 123, 124–5

Report on Special Educational Needs (1978) 1, 2, 9; and maladjustment 2; and planning 11–12

schools: child management in 154–69; creative subjects in 160; groupwork in 164; and mediated learning 162–5; management and the curriculum 158–62; organization of 156, 163; physical education in 160; special 143–5, 146–8; therapeutic approaches in 165–8; *see also* learning difficulties, Report on Special Educational Needs, special educational needs, special schools

sexual abuse; *see* physical/sexual abuse

sexual development in childhood 28–9, 31–2

social-learning theory 42, 47

special educational needs 158–62 *passim; see also* learning difficulties

special schools 168; and behaviourist approaches 167–8; case-studies in placement 143–5, 146–8; 'token economy' in 168

transference: case-study of 107–8; negative 107–8; positive 107; in psychoanalytic psychotherapy 106–8

Warnock Report 154–5

Winnicott, D. W.: on child development 37–8; on mother–child relations 37–8; on object relations 37